Build Wealth With Common Stocks

Self-improvement books by David J. Waldron:

Hire Train Monitor Motivate

The Ten Domains of Effective Goal Setting

Build Wealth With Common Stocks

Market-Beating Strategies for the Individual Investor

David J. Waldron

Country View

Country View
https://davidjwaldron.com
Carlisle, Pennsylvania, USA

Portions of this book contain original material written by the author and first published on the investing website Seeking Alpha.

First Edition
21   8 3 1

Cover design by Robin Johnson
Interior design created with IngramSpark Book-Building Tool

Disclaimer: This book is intended solely for education and illustration. The author/publisher neither implies nor guarantees success as individual circumstances and, therefore, results vary.

ISBN: 978-1-7355524-0-8 (hc)
ISBN: 978-1-7355524-1-5 (sc)

Library of Congress Control Number: 2020914998

For Suzan, in dedication to your enduring love and for teaching me the principles of living a quality and valued life.

CONTENTS █

CONTENTS

ACKNOWLEDGMENTS ▌

This first edition of *Build Wealth with Common Stocks* is far superior to my draft manuscript thanks to the dedication, moral support, and constructive feedback of the advance reader team: Shonna Dent, James Devine, Christina Gaza, Bud Joyner, Justin Loidolt, Mariska Mosterd-van Wijnen, Ram Persaud, Carolyn Waldron, Rob Weiss, and special recognition to Rick Urquhart, for his above-and-beyond contributions.

I also extend gratitude to the dedicated professionals, organizations, and publications for the direct support or indirect influence on the editing, design, publishing, marketing, and legal guidance in making this book possible: ACX, Authorgraph, BookFunnel, Stephanie Chandler, *The Chicago Manual of Style*, Draft2Digital, Grammarly, Gene Hutnak Photography, IngramSpark, Evan Jacobs, Robin Johnson, Kindle Direct Publishing, Robin Ludwig Design, NetGalley, Nonfiction Authors Association, Karl W. Palachuk, Heather Pendley, Leander Potters, Reedsy, Helen Sedwick, Seeking Alpha, Daniel Shvartsman, TalkMarkets, and a special nod of gratefulness to the late authors William Strunk, Jr., and E.B. White for the indispensable classic *The Elements of Style*.

Whether by service or inspiration, the contributions of each individual and organization to this work are cherished and appreciated. I believe the reader has wholly benefited from your immeasurable talents and invaluable resources.

B *uild Wealth with Common Stocks* is an individual investor-centered book using a well-planned and executed model portfolio of total-return common stocks as a real-time case study on the merits of buy-and-hold, value-based, retail-level investing. The book is for the everyday investor seeking to build or maintain a portfolio with the goal of funding significant milestones in life, such as buying a home, paying for a college education, pursuing a passion, starting a business, or enjoying a comfortable retirement.

Build Wealth with Common Stocks speaks to the retail investor who is thoughtful about the continuous improvement of investment wisdom; disciplined to conduct the due diligence toward discovering quality, publicly traded companies with common shares exhibiting wide margins of safety; and patient in waiting for the compounding of capital gains and dividends to build personal wealth over time.

If this opening is hitting home, you are encouraged to read the book and join an investment community dedicated to finding value and building wealth without subsidizing the Wall Street fee machine.

The Reader Best Served

Any individual investor, regardless of a specific niche, is encouraged to read the book as the pursuit of excellence in long-term, buy-and-hold common stock investing is broad in scope. Although the book welcomes every investor to participate and benefit, the platform best serves the following pre-retirement retail investor profiles.

- An investor who is seeking to open or maintain existing personal brokerage or tax-deferred accounts, such as a 401(k), 403(b), individual retirement account (IRA), Roth IRA, or 529 tuition plan. The investor wants to establish or build upon a self-managed, buy-and-hold investing approach to personal money management.

- An investor who retains professional money management, such as an investment advisor, broker/dealer, financial planner, or who relies on a family member to oversee their brokerage or tax-deferred investment portfolios. The investor wants to improve an understanding of the process of active portfolio management, thereby facilitating valuable communication with and adequate oversight of the money manager.

- An investor who enjoys acquiring new ideas to meet the everyday challenges of personal finance. Money is often a taboo discussion in our lives; therefore, *Build Wealth with Common Stocks* is designed as a straightforward and safety-minded vehicle to explore the thoughts, ideas, and challenges of do-it-yourself investing. It is expected the investor will disagree with or outright dismiss some of the principles, strategies, and practices shared in this book; the intent is to take what is needed and to leave the rest.

- An investor already committed to—or with a keen interest in—the value investing model of buying dividend-paying common shares of excellent businesses when trading at reasonable prices. The value model was invented by the late Columbia Business School professors Benjamin Graham and David Dodd and made famous by professional investors Warren Buffett, William Browne, Joel Greenblatt, Seth Klarman, Peter Lynch, Howard Marks, John W. Rogers Jr., Charles Royce, Geraldine Weiss, and Martin Whitman, among other legends.

What to Expect from *Build Wealth with Common Stocks*

This book aims to create value for the reader by centering on how to screen, research, and select potential ownership slices of publicly traded companies offering enduring legacies to stakeholders, inclusive of customers, employees, vendors, suppliers, regulators, the community at large, and present or future shareholders.

Out of respect for the reader, *Build Wealth with Common Stocks* rejects any short-term trading schemes for hopeful—although improbable—quick financial gains using controversial investment vehicles. Hence, the book discourages options, futures, event arbitrage, currencies—whether crypto or sovereign—commodities, trend following, short-selling, technical analysis, swing trading, momentum growth, high-yield dividends, price targets and alerts, trading algorithms, margin accounts, deep value, or any trading schemes deployed in the hopes of acquiring fast money. The author concedes those speculative ventures to professional traders, market gamblers, and the Ouija board.

Also absent is investment advice directed to the unique financial situation of the reader. Per securities laws and regulations, the text must maintain an impersonal narrative. The book is devoted to sharing broad ideas based on the author's personal experience. Consider the author an educator and well-intended enabler—as opposed to a stock market guru—for the benefit of the do-it-yourself everyday investor.

As of the writing of this Introduction, the author's real-time family portfolio had been outperforming its benchmark since June 2009 by a significant average margin of each representative holding. The market-beating performance continued during the COVID-19 coronavirus pandemic that rendered the stock market as volatile and unpredictable as the financial crisis and Great Recession of 2008–2009.

Principles, Strategies, and Practices

Self-directed common stock investing is simple, although never easy; doable, albeit intimidating. Uncomplicated, focused research conducted with thought, discipline, and patience has more significant potential to outperform the market over an extended holding period. Whimsical references to "the market" throughout the book represent the aggregate of fickle retail and aggressive professional investors who are lost in the crowd and ruled by emotions or greed in the day-to-day buying and selling of investment securities.

Build Wealth with Common Stocks presents several principles, strategies, and practices of profitable investing that, when implemented with consistency by the long-view, individual investor, have the potential to produce a market-beating portfolio. During twenty plus years of active investing, the author discovered several essential standards—shared in Part I: Principles—that when merged with a handful of fundamental measures of a company, often pointed in the general direction of the forward-looking, long-term performance of the underlying stock.

In Part II: Strategies, the author analyzes several areas of a company and its common shares. His simplified research methodologies identify the value proposition, quantify shareholder returns, measure management effectiveness, weigh the intrinsic value of the stock, and assess the overall downside risk. Ruled out are companies presenting as lacking in more than a few of these targeted traits.

Part III: Practices pulls the principles and strategies of Part I and Part II together for the reader toward building a potential market-beating, well-allocated, low-cost, common stock portfolio.

From this book, you will learn how to exercise a bottom-up research approach that acknowledges and accounts for stakeholders in the company, including the board of directors and senior management. You will treat the market as a stakeholder as well, if only for a contradictory confirmation of your investment thesis.

By focusing research on fantastic companies with ethical management generating consistent, organic revenue growth, sustained profitability, and high returns on working capital, market-beating portfolios are possible for the thoughtful, retail-level Main Street investor. Become the investor who buys and holds the common shares of great businesses producing quality products and services for customers, as well as generating long-term, total return in capital appreciation and income for the shareholder.

Are you ready to apply market-beating principles and strategies such as presented in *Build Wealth with Common Stocks* in your workplace or individual retirement accounts, tuition savings plan, or taxable brokerage account?

Do you have the ingredients necessary to succeed as a retail-level common stock investor through each market cycle?

Read on, as you probably have the innate ability to succeed or are already applying many of the principles and strategies with opportunities to further improve your success as an individual investor. A primary objective of this book is to facilitate self-awareness and fill in the blanks as warranted.

The Model Portfolio

The Model Portfolio is equal-weighted—each holding has the same prorata amount invested—against the broader market benchmark based on the dates of the initial common stock purchase or the original publication of the underlying research. Past performance is never an indicator of future returns.

The Model Portfolio is an abridged, illustrative benchmark gauging the financial and business metrics of a concentrated basket of the common shares of publicly traded companies that constituted an actively managed core family portfolio at the time of writing this edition of the book.

Portfolio updates average several key financial indicators at each quarter- and year-end close. The model provides a comparative analysis and overall performance of the representative companies using the financial and business metrics discussed in Part II: Strategies.

Disclosures

At the time of this writing, the author's real-time family portfolio—as illustrated in the public version, The Model Portfolio—had long positions in the common shares of the following companies and exchange-traded funds mentioned in this edition of the book (exchange: ticker symbol) — Apple, Inc. (NASDAQ: AAPL), Comcast Corporation (NASDAQ: CMCSA), CVS Health Corporation (NYSE: CVS), The Walt Disney Company (NYSE: DIS), The Coca-Cola Company (NYSE: KO), Johnson & Johnson (NYSE: JNJ), The Kroger Company (NYSE: KR), Southwest Airlines Co. (NYSE: LUV), 3M Company (NYSE: MMM), Microsoft Corporation (NASDAQ: MSFT), Nike, Inc. (NYSE: NKE), The TJX Companies, Inc. (NYSE: TJX), Toyota Motor Corporation (NYSE ADR: TM), Union Pacific Corporation (NYSE: UNP), and Vanguard FTSE All-World ex-US Index Fund ETF Shares (NYSE: VEU).

Other than owning shares of common stock and consuming some of the products or services, the author and his immediate family have no other business relationship with the publicly traded companies mentioned. The author may add or remove positions from his family portfolio without public disclosure. To follow the activity of The Model Portfolio, take advantage of a complimentary reader membership at davidjwaldron.com. Please note the free membership option may change or discontinue at any time without notice.

Additional Disclosures

This book presents source material as general information for reference by the interested reader. The accuracy of the data cannot be guaranteed. Narrative and analytics are impersonal and neither tailored to individual needs nor intended for portfolio construction beyond the author's model portfolio presented solely for illustration. The author is an individual investor and not an investment advisor. It is the responsibility of the reader to engage in independent research. Consider consulting, if appropriate, a fee-only certified financial planner, licensed discount broker/dealer, flat-fee registered investment advisor, certified public accountant, or specialized attorney before making any investment, income tax, or estate planning decisions.

Disclaimers

The Model Portfolio provides a nondiversified, narrow snapshot of author-owned collective company components for comparative research. It is neither a marketable security nor intended for investment advice or portfolio construction. Present and past illustrative performances of The Model Portfolio are neither a guarantee of actual or future performance of its constituent companies, sectors, and industries nor the stock market as a whole.

The Model Portfolio is owned, maintained, and published for the primary financial benefit of the author's immediate family and second as an educational platform for the active members of his website. It is forbidden to copy, market, benchmark, or disseminate The Model Portfolio without the express written permission of the author.

It is expected that the reader understands and accepts the disclosures and disclaimers written in this Introduction before reading the entirety of the book. By implementing any of the principles and strategies shared in the book, the reader accepts full liability for any investing failures or missed expectations. The reader alone is responsible for personal financial decisions.

Financial Services Industry

Although the book takes a skeptical view of Wall Street—a euphemism of professional or institutional investing anywhere in the world—it neither implies nor expresses specific issues with or negative references to any actual organizations or individuals existing or working in the financial services industry. Any perceived reference or offense to actual firms or real persons is coincidental and unintentional. In its general lament of the Wall Street way, the book abstains from unproven conspiracy theories and instead presents a narrative nonfiction platform of commentary, critique, education, and parody.

In the world at large, facts are indeed exempt from any alternative paradigm; thus, the subjective thoughts shared by the author throughout the book are his opinions and, therefore, independent from fact.

Trademarks

Companies often declare trademarks as designations to distinguish products. All brand names and product names used in this book are trade names, service marks, or registered trademarks of the owners. The author/publisher is not associated with any product or vendor mentioned in this book. Unless featured with permission on the cover or in approved marketing messages, none of the individuals or organizations referenced within the text have endorsed the book.

Gender Neutrality

The principles, strategies, and practices presented throughout the book apply to all genders equally. In the interest of clarity and consistency, the author uses gender-neutral pronouns in the text.

Links to Author's Website and Model Portfolio

Although posted in the book with intended restraint, links to the author's website are free to the public. The reader understands the author assumes no responsibility or liability for any damages from electronic viruses that may occur from accessing any websites listed or implied in the book, such as researching investment-related material. The author has no responsibility for the persistence or accuracy of URLs for external or third-party internet websites referred to or implied in this book and does not guarantee that any content on such sites is, or will remain, accurate or appropriate.

Access to The Model Portfolio and other exclusive member resources are complementary to readers choosing to join the author's mailing list at davidjwaldron.com. The author makes a living on passive earnings such as investment-related capital gains and dividends, book royalties, website display advertising, and affiliate marketing. If you find value in the read, please post a review at your site of purchase, recommend the book to a colleague, friend, or family member, or buy a copy at your favorite bookstore to gift someone special.

For the Benefit of the Reader

In Part III: Chapter Sixteen, under the section titled "Stock Screen User Guide and Definitions," you will find an annotated glossary of several of the investing terms presented in the book. The reader is encouraged to bookmark that section in advance and refer to it as needed.

In deference to the proliferation of book abstracts in publishing, each chapter concludes with a bulleted summary. You are encouraged to use the lists for review or clarification while reading and for quick reference later.

Welcome to *Build Wealth with Common Stocks*

The investment principles, strategies, and practices shared throughout the book were cultivated from the author's more than twenty years of learning and practicing the growth and preservation of wealth from self-directed investing. *Build Wealth with Common Stocks* is a sincere and enthusiastic attempt at sharing a personal experience with readers from every level of the retail spectrum toward mutual investment nirvana from the magic of compounding protected by a wide margin of safety.

Remember, if you benefit from the read, please post a review where you purchased the book. For general questions or to offer constructive feedback, please write the author at info@davidjwaldron.com.

* * *

INTRODUCTION SUMMARY

On Taking Stock and Responsibility

- *Build Wealth with Common Stocks* is for the everyday investor seeking to build or maintain a portfolio toward funding significant milestones in life.

- Any investor is encouraged to read the book as the pursuit of excellence in long-term, buy-and-hold common stock investing is broad in scope, where every level of investor participates with the potential to prosper.

- *Build Wealth with Common Stocks* rejects any nearsighted trading schemes for hopeful—although improbable—quick financial gains.

- This book is limited to information and illustration. The accuracy of the data cannot be guaranteed. Narrative and analytics are impersonal — neither tailored to individual needs nor intended for portfolio construction beyond The Model Portfolio presented within the limitations of teaching and learning. The author is an individual investor, not an investment advisor. It is the responsibility of the reader to engage in independent research and consider consulting a licensed professional before making any investment, income tax, or estate planning decisions.

- For the benefit of the reader, Part III: Chapter Sixteen defines several investing terms used in the book, and each chapter concludes with a bulleted summary for review and reference.

I

PRINCIPLES

One

Get Rich Slow

An informed investor has a far greater chance of getting rich slow than getting rich fast, and getting rich slowly is better than not at all.

Build Wealth with Common Stocks—my fourth book—provides investment principles and portfolio strategies for the retail investor who wants to uncover the dividend-paying common stocks of quality companies to benefit from the compounding shares of those enterprises.

I have done just that through four market cycles and counting.

My objective as an author is to teach what I know and to learn what I don't. Since my crystal ball cracked years ago, I strive to practice honest and prudent investing in an impulsive world, thereby creating value for our family's investment portfolio.*

The do-it-yourself common stock investor beats the market over time with thought, discipline, and patience by sticking to a simple menu of time-tested, winning principles and strategies. It is now your opportunity to invest alongside me as a peer retail-level investor. I have persevered and profited despite some of the rockiest markets in our recent history: the dot-com implosion of the early 2000s, the financial crisis of 2008–09, the epic post-Great Recession bull-market era, and the volatility-driven activity from the COVID-19 coronavirus pandemic of 2020.

* * *

*References to "our family portfolio" represent the combined individual and joint investment accounts of my household.

Building a Market-Beating Portfolio

In this book, you will learn how to profit from time-tested market-beating principles and strategies from a real-time actively managed model portfolio constructed with a concentrated blend of total-return common stocks. Members of my author website have exclusive, ongoing access to the key financial indicators of our family portfolio—shared as The Model Portfolio—in a user-friendly spreadsheet updated at each quarter- and year-end. The updates include a narrative report, another member exclusive, highlighting the performance and developments of the holdings of the portfolio.

The Model Portfolio encompasses the common shares of high-conviction, dividend-paying quality enterprises, with a few sometimes trading at value prices. My proprietary daily performance tracker—also a member exclusive—provides real-time tracking of The Model Portfolio and highlights the overall performance of the individual common stock holdings against the S&P 500 benchmark, an index of the largest publicly traded companies available on the major US stock exchanges. A portfolio spreadsheet, released quarterly, further measures performance in quarter-to-date, one-year, and since-inception periods.

As an accompaniment to the principles and strategies discussed throughout the book, you are encouraged to access The Model Portfolio with my compliments by joining the member list at my SSL-secured author website, davidjwaldron.com.

Track Record

After getting earnest about value-based common stock investing, the shares of the publicly traded companies invested in our family portfolio of taxable and tax-deferred accounts had beat the S&P 500 Index by a decisive margin, based on average per holding since its inception in June 2009. During those eleven years leading to the publishing of this book, the cumulative equal-weighted average total return of each of the holdings of The Model Portfolio, as of the period ending June 30, 2020, had outperformed the S&P 500 by +6,749 basis points (bps), the equivalent to an average of +67.49 percentage points per holding.

Build Wealth with Common Stocks underscores market-beating potential over a long-term holding period as opposed to next week, next month, or a year from now. As of the market close on June 30, 2020—following the market freefall and subsequent seesawing from the coronavirus pandemic—the performance of The Model Portfolio had affirmed the benefits of a longer-view investment paradigm.

For example, although the six stocks held fewer than three years in the portfolio were underperforming the S&P 500 by an average of -2,009 bps per holding or -20.09 percentage points, the six held between three and five years were outperforming the benchmark by an average of +2,170 bps or +21.70 percentage points. And the five stocks held for longer than five years were beating the S&P 500 by a resounding +22,752 bps average per holding or +227.52 percentage points each on average.

Investors who give up on underperforming stocks held fewer than three or four years forego the potential for a sizable market outperformance after five or more years of compounding. The Model Portfolio has demonstrated the time-tested investment platform of buy-and-hold value investing is alive, well, and here to stay.

Methodology

For a more balanced view of the performances of each holding, The Model Portfolio is equal-weighted against the S&P 500 Index based on the dates of my initial stock purchase or the original publication of the research. Total return represents the stock price performance adjusted for splits and dividends. Past performance is unrelated to future returns.

The public version of our family portfolio showcased throughout the book serves as a metaphor for building a low-cost, lesser-risk, and perhaps market-beating portfolio, despite any limits of available investment capital. Supported by a daily portfolio tracker and quarterly report of performance and opportunities, The Model Portfolio is an actively managed, real-time portfolio of major US exchange-traded common stocks using a proprietary research system.

The Vision of The Model Portfolio

Every venture, including a self-managed investment portfolio, ought to have a vision statement. Below is the concept behind The Model Portfolio.

> Long-term investment horizon, buying slices of quality, dividend-paying companies at reasonable prices, and holding the investment for as long as the company remains wonderful, including forever.

I am an advocate of investing in great companies producing in-demand and profitable products or services that are assisting consumers worldwide in solving personal and business problems, wants, or needs.

The profitable common stock portfolio resembles a collection of owned slices of companies producing high-quality products or services with enduring competitive advantages. As far as trading stocks, the retail investor who is inclined to gamble drops by the local casino with discretionary dollars and, whether winning or losing, has a good time. The disciplined investor never places bets on investment tips or perceived opportunities for quick, wishful gains.

Value Investing Defined

Defining value investing is an arduous task and is forever debated in financial media. The do-it-yourself investor favors simplicity over sophistication. Believing that value investing is the purest, most productive form of common stock investing, I give our family portfolio and the concepts supporting each investment a symbolic kiss.

KISS — Keep Investing Super Simple.

The definition of value investing is steadfast to the word value as it applies to every aspect of our consuming lives, including investments. Here is how Merriam-Webster.com defines *value*:

> *Amount of money that something is worth.*
> *Price or cost of something.*
> *Something that can be bought for a lower or fair price.*
> *Usefulness or importance of something.[1]*

An analysis of common stocks is quite similar to purchase considerations in other aspects of our lives.

What is the product or service worth to us? What is the quoted price? What is the difference between the two, and will the product or service be available for a lower or fairer price point in the future? Put another way, is it cheap based on the inherent value we place on the product or service? Just as important, why buy a cheap product or service unless we find usefulness or importance in owning the product or service?

Now substitute company or stock for a product or service and re-read the same paragraph based on the formal definition of value.

What is the company worth to us? What is the quoted stock price? What is the difference between the two, and will it be available for a lower or fairer price point in the future? Put another way, is it cheap based on the inherent worth we place on the enterprise? Just as important, why buy a cheap stock unless we see usefulness or importance in owning a slice of the business?

Value investing endures as the simplest of investment strategies in a complex financial services industry.

The Objective of *Build Wealth with Common Stocks*

Now apply the above formal definition of *value* to an investment philosophy.

> Buy and hold the common shares of US exchange-traded, dividend-paying, well-managed, financially sound businesses that produce easy-to-understand products or services, have enduring competitive advantages from wide economic moats, enjoy steady, free cash flow, and are trading at a discount to the investor's perceived intrinsic value at the time of purchase. Next, of utmost importance and perhaps the biggest challenge, practice patience in waiting for the investment thesis to play out as projected over a long-term horizon.

My suggested objective or investment philosophy of the retail investor is short, to the point, and focused on quality products and services. Built-in barriers to competition are produced and sold by financially sound companies represented by the underlying common shares. First, purchase targeted securities at fair, reasonable, or cheap prices. Then hold for as long as your conviction is confirmed by the performances of the company and its stock.

How do you measure the quality of the products or services of a business, its competitive advantages, financial strengths, the perceived enduring value relative to the stock price, and the downside risk?

Keep investing super simple by limiting your measurement and analysis to a handful of essential metrics in each critical area of the enterprise, such as competitive advantages, returns to shareholders, management effectiveness, the intrinsic value of the stock, and the combined risk profile of the company and its common shares.

Indeed, due diligence in The Model Portfolio involves profiling the fundamentals of the selected company with counter understanding and acceptance of the downside risk, were the thesis or measure of intrinsic value to misfire. Using proprietary screens encompassing the above metrics, I actively manage individual common stock investments in The Model Portfolio and share the performance and trends with members via the exclusive daily position trackers and quarterly narrative reports. The analysis in each report follows the general outline shared in this book for a concise, easy-to-read, and understandable information flow tying together each portfolio holding. Part II: Strategies presents the five methodologies in detail.

Being forever reminded that markets go up and down at a moment's notice, you have to start somewhere. Thus, members of davidjwaldron.com are informed about the targeted common shares of publicly traded companies added, held, or removed from The Model Portfolio, for better or worse. Template-driven research does annoy some readers, although the value in working from a flexible outline is the consistency and discipline it brings to your investing acumen.

Modest doses of thought, discipline, and patience, plus a pinch of common sense, produced a market-beating basket of common stocks in The Model Portfolio for eleven years running as of June 2020.

The Mission of *Build Wealth with Common Stocks*

The book's philosophical goal is for the reader to experience an empathetic journey long and positive on self-paced financial education, mutual respect, and a shared passion for buy-and-hold investment excellence. And short and cynical of know-it-all gurus, disregard for the counter opinions of others, and get-rich-quick trading schemes.

My purpose behind writing *Build Wealth with Common Stocks* is to provide an actionable portfolio strategy prescribing a proven set of core methodologies for the benefit of the wealth-building investor, as defined by its mission.

Mission

The mission of *Build Wealth with Common Stocks* and The Model Portfolio:

> Facilitate a community of thoughtful, disciplined, and patient everyday investors who are passionate about learning, practicing, and sharing the art and science of building wealth from the magic of compounding, protected by a wide margin of safety.

Owning the common shares of world-class enterprises builds winning portfolios over time from the compounding total return of capital gains and dividends. *Build Wealth with Common Stocks*—as illustrated in The Model Portfolio—is committed to the strict bottom-up, buy-and-hold value investing paradigm. It avoids price targets, price alerts, technical charts, deep-dive analysis paralysis, top-down macro influence, momentum or trend investing, market-timing, short-selling, options trading, high-yield dividends, and trade set-ups.

The book is limited to advocating the long-term, low-fee ownership of the dividend-paying common shares of quality companies. I do enjoy sharing successes—and failures—with fellow retail investors as we are in this together for better and perhaps worse, although never on speculation. The loved ones who benefit from our investment pursuits deserve more than the speculative flavors of the month emanating out of the Wall Street fee machine.

And we deserve better.

Mine Relevant Data and Exercise Self-Control

The successful, retail-level investor mines relevant data, exercises self-control, and applies tenacity to portfolio construction and maintenance, eschewing complicated or expensive investment vehicles or any trading schemes in the hopes of fast money. The profitable, independent investor is happy to leave those speculative ventures to professional traders and market gamblers.

To its credit, the financial services industry has rolled out versions of KISS—keep investing super simple—such as discounted or commission-free online brokerages and low-cost index funds. Nonetheless, investors suppress any advantages from discounted or free commissions by trading on margin or too often, thereby risking unnecessary debt, trading fees, and tax burdens on what was supposed to be a low-cost experience.

Active and Passive Investing in One Approach

Employing an invest-it-and-forget-it style is an ideal variant for the passive S&P 500 Index investor. *Build Wealth with Common Stocks* is for the thoughtful investor who wants to merge the lower cost and lesser risk of passive investing—via hedging—with the potential for above-average returns from active buy-and-hold investing. The active investor enjoys picking and managing investments through rigorous education and discipline.

Although hedging is a complex paradigm of investing, in the context of this book, it represents a simple long position in a portfolio, such as an S&P 500 benchmark or similar index exchange-traded fund (ETF), to reduce the risk exposure of common stocks from the inevitable market gyrations. Chapter Eight discusses the practical concept of portfolio hedging.

Using an active approach to investing, hedged by passive indexes, The Model Portfolio has proven that getting rich slow by outperforming the market over the long-term is possible on Main Street and is an enjoyable and self-actualizing experience.

Welcome to *Build Wealth with Common Stocks*. May you enjoy and benefit from the book as much as I enjoyed writing it from the experience of implementing the principles and strategies in our family portfolio over an extended holding period.

* * *

CHAPTER ONE SUMMARY

On Getting Rich Slowly

- The do-it-yourself common stock investor beats the market over time with thought, discipline, and patience by sticking to a simple menu of time-tested, winning principles and strategies.

- Value investing endures as the simplest of investment strategies in a complex financial services industry.

- Consider giving your portfolio a symbolic kiss and keep investing super simple.

- Subscribe to The Model Portfolio with my compliments at david-jwaldron.com.

- An informed investor has a far greater chance of getting rich slow than getting rich fast, and getting rich slowly is better than not at all.

Two

Filter The Noise

I outperformed the S&P 500 over time by filtering the noise on Wall Street and avoiding the risk-heavy high flyers or trading schemes of the moment. This chapter addresses the financial services industry's captive influence on the Main Street investor and how to sift through the inherent bias.

Lessons in Street Noise Reduction

The economist John Kenneth Galbraith said, "We have two classes of forecasters: Those who don't know, and those who don't know they don't know."[1]

Too many investors believe it is possible to predict trends, catalysts, and macro events with consistency. Crystal balls, disguised in sophisticated methodologies, encapsulate forward revenues and earnings projections as well as specific future stock prices. Indeed, history shows such practices are the fool's game.

A tiny percentage of investors are wired with the emotional intelligence to make winning short-term trades—such as 60/40 win-loss rates or similar—more often than most market participants. A few of these gifted traders sell the schemes to a public thirsty for fast money. Nevertheless, science has yet to discover how to transfer the DNA code of successful traders to customers. On its own, the shortsighted strategy underperforms what was promised or hoped.

Despite a significant shortfall in brain wiring, we want it to work for the sake of the financial security of our family. Thus, we keep going back for more quick money ideas, perhaps from a different source blessed with market-timing DNA, although our misaligned intent remains. In fairness, the purveyor is often a well-intentioned market whiz kid trying to spread the gospel of what appears as easy money. Again and again, we revisit the dry well despite lacking the harness necessary to time the market, reassured from the expectation that another swath of fast money wannabes will join us at the next market fad roll-out party.

The nineteenth century circus impresario, P. T. Barnum, uncovered this unrelenting human fallacy over 150 years ago. Paraphrased by a captivated media from his notorious carnival barking, Barnum implied there's a sucker born every minute. His legendary reference to poor judgment still applies years later, and the stock market is no exception. The good news is such market-wide irrational behavior creates profitable buying opportunities, if only temporarily, providing the potential to outperform the market over time.

Invest valued time in your portfolio instead of languishing it by following the pundits. Leave the daily noise and prognostications to the captivated followers of the small group of DNA-blessed market experts and technicians. Each keeps readers, viewers, or listeners entertained as portfolios implode from inadequate allocations influenced by the trading nonsense filling the Wall Street vacuum daily. Take heed of the talking heads, including me, as an author, for the sake and safety of your portfolio.

This book is neither about recent market conditions nor what I was buying, selling, holding, shorting, or exploiting to outwit the market in the short term, leaving that chatterbox to the financial entertainers. It is about muting the noise emanating from Wall Street and keeping investing super simple by taking advantage of the time-tested winning strategy of buying slices of blue-chip companies and then holding each for the long-term as a proud shareholder.

The Fast Money Paradigm

In general, investors are seeking short-term bursts of growth-driven capital gains and high-yield dividend income. The crowd wants instant gratification from the implied promises of promoted trading platforms that, based on historical results, more often underperform the market. The incongruity reminds us that on Wall Street, the crowd is almost always wrong, or average at best, across market cycles.

Powered by Ivy League degrees and sophisticated software, Wall Street disseminates complex, assumptive financial models of precision earnings estimates and price targets each market day. Many of those projections play out as no more intuitive than a Magic 8-Ball, or else the financial services elite is accumulating wealth from portfolio performance as much as from fees and bonuses. Like clockwork, the herd investor asks, "At what specific price will the stock be trading next week, next year, and in the year 2029?"

My answer: I don't know. I do know that investing in common stocks to take advantage of the magic of compounding protected by a wide margin of safety—next up in Chapter Three—presents an ideal scenario for portfolio success over a lifetime, in contrast to a single bull market. Nonetheless, deep-dive research is overrated. If superior at predicting future stock prices, why isn't every investor wealthy from following the stock picks of fund managers and the price targets of sell-side or buy-side analysts, each a purveyor of the deep-dive approach?

It is impossible to predict market directions with consistency or within specific dates and time frames. Just ask the short-sellers left with their shorts down for the decade of 2010 to 2019. The successful forecast of a particular market downturn occurs at random from a few lucky calls by the pundits, who are then placed on a pedestal by the Wall Street media and guru-of-the-month trading clubs. Nevertheless, corrections occur at unknown points in time, and thus, anyone who predicts a market drop or pop, in general, gets to be right.

Hit or Miss?

In a former career, I hosted hedge and mutual fund managers as well as sell-side analysts at a publicly traded company that employed me as an executive. I enjoyed the experience and had great respect for the visitors. A few of these professional investors now enjoy celebrity status in financial media. I wondered about the value our guests had gained from kicking the tires as my employer cultivated everything shared during the visits. Perhaps the outing was an intuitive experience for the fund managers and analysts?

The resulting investments or calls on the stock of the company were more often wrong. The message from this enlightening experience is for the Main Street investor to mute the Wall Street quantitative analysts, traders, and high-profile money managers focused on sophisticated activities intended to generate short-term gains for clients and followers.

Wall Street lives and dies by its quarterly earnings releases and the fanfare preceding and following each report. Forecasting future stock prices, market movements, revenue growth, or earnings per share (EPS) with consistent accuracy is arbitrary, even from senior management of a company. I never attempt to predict in detail what will happen with the stock market or any particular business. Instead, I screen, research, and monitor quality businesses for mispriced value. My intent is for this book to inspire you to join in the quest for similar investing nirvana. Strive to study and learn in the short term as you save and invest for the long term.

The lesson is about owning slices of excellent companies as opposed to trading speculative instruments. This book attempts to answer why and how putting quality before speculation is the more profitable approach to retail investing.

Limited Capital but Lower Costs and Less Risk

Despite limited capital, the individual investor on Main Street has the potential to achieve superior long-term percentage returns with lower costs and less risk than the power brokers working on Wall Street. To be sure, Wall Street outperforms Main Street in overall investment-related income because of its knack for punishing clients with enormous churns of fees and commissions. As contrarians of the Wall Street way, the mantra of the Main Street common stock investor is the absolute return of both capital gains and dividends with minimal fees and commissions.

It seems everything I tend to avoid is what the crowd seeks, as influenced by the Wall Street fee-generating propaganda machine. Our family portfolio outperformed the S&P 500 using the investment principles and strategies shared in these pages. It became the primary motivation for writing the book, thereby compelling me to share what has worked for my family with you and yours.

Counteracting the overall failure of Wall Street to its Main Street constituents, the book is about building and maintaining a low-cost, less-risk, common stock portfolio with market-beating potential over an extended holding period, regardless of available capital. The do-it-yourself investor committed to managing a portfolio without the exclusive use of a professional investment advisor or high-cost investment service, and, with more self-directed means such as online discount brokers, investment bloggers or podcasters, and low-cost subscription services, is encouraged to use this book as one of those resources.

The *Build Wealth with Common Stocks* Creed

The creed of *Build Wealth with Common Stocks* mirrors the wisdom of legendary investor Warren Buffett—founder and chairman of Berkshire Hathaway, Inc. (NYSE: BRK.A, BRK.B)—the premier investor of our time who happens to live and work in Omaha, Nebraska, instead of Manhattan, New York.

“ The "know-nothing" investor who both diversifies and keeps ”
his costs minimal is virtually certain to get satisfactory re-
sults. Indeed, the unsophisticated investor who is realistic
about his shortcomings is likely to obtain better long-term re-
sults than the knowledgeable professional who is blind to even
a single weakness.[2]

—WARREN BUFFETT

Buffett wrote the profound quote in his 2013 letter to Berkshire Hathaway shareholders. He proposes the inexperienced investor who is being pragmatic about imperfections is in a position to obtain better long-term results than the informed, although shortsighted, professional. The successful investor on Main Street is aware of the inherent shortcomings that, in the eyes of the Wall Street elite, equate to an unsophisticated, know-nothing amateur. As suggested in the wisdom of Buffett, combine the alleged impaired vision of investment insight with common sense, low-cost, risk-conscious asset allocation within your investment model.

The return horizon is the slow and steady long-view in opposition to the get-rich-quick mentality of the day trader, trend follower, or momentum investor.

The Juxtaposition of Wall Street

Within movie-making jargon, juxtaposing is the art of presenting two opposing ideas or characters in contrast to each other within a scene or storyline. If successful, the juxtaposition creates an illusion pulling the viewer into the director's vision. Such is the value of entertainment. Whether it is worth the ten bucks per ticket and double that for popcorn, candy, and soft drinks depends on the movie. Nonetheless, many films fail to recoup budgets despite the high costs passed on to viewers. Movies are risky investments, indeed.

On Wall Street, the coupling of superb investment return potential—or the recorded history of actual returns—and high fee structures
presents as a lucrative juxtaposition. Such hubris creates an illusion of
justified elevated costs to participating investors from projected or historical returns created by higher educated and credentialed professionals.

Unlike the movies, there are no scripted endings or guaranteed outcomes in investing. Just as a talented film director creating art, the titans
of Wall Street generate record-breaking revenue streams by way of enormous fees and commissions coupled with legal mirages of the potential
for superb investment returns. Wall Street has crafted the art of making
investing a sophisticated institution, thereby justifying overspending for
results that underperform in many scenarios.

The Wall Street way tempts a movie director's quest for an entertaining juxtaposition. Just ask Oliver Stone, co-writer and director of the
classic drama *Wall Street*,[3] featuring Michael Douglas as the antagonist
Gordon Gekko, an unscrupulous corporate raider. Douglas won a best
actor Academy Award for his archetypal portrayal of the 1980's excess.

Outperforming Gordon Gekko

As reported on a widespread basis in the financial media, perhaps a
minority of Wall Street traders and money managers beat the market
with consistency; the market defined as the S&P 500 or any asset class
the particular investment product benchmarks. It seems that collecting
fees and commissions along with leveraging assets under management
is what finances the annual profit and bonus windfalls on Wall Street
more than its investment returns. If a majority of professional portfolio
managers underperform the market, why does the collective of individual and institutional investors continue to pour trillions of dollars into
the advisory fee sucking coffers?

Perhaps it is all we know. The Wall Street way induces the customer
to its mode of thinking via slick advertising campaigns, press release re-

gurgitation from mainstream print and online media, and the proverbial talking heads on financial television stations. And the
well-intentioned human resource department at our employer steers
us into high-priced one-size-fits-all retirement plans and risky company
stock with an unknowing smile of loyalty to the status quo.

Then again, why argue with success in the era of the billionaire class
and paparazzi pervaded celebrities?

Who's Driving the Sports Car?

There is an adage that says never take advice from a salesperson, yet investors let Wall Street institutions sell them biased information all day
long. Imagine going to an upscale restaurant one weeknight to celebrate
your significant other's birthday or job promotion. At the end of the
evening, as you are waiting for the valet to bring up your vehicle, you
notice a $150,000 sports car already in the queue awaiting its driver. It
has vanity plates, so the next day your internet search of the name on the
plate uncovers the owner of the luxury vehicle as a local independent financial planner affiliated with a national investment and insurance brokerage.

An online profile seems to portray the financial planner as a decent
citizen, and the sponsoring investment advisory services company shows
no apparent issues in a related internet search. It is evident the financial
planner sells high commission products such as annuities, whole life insurance, complex trusts, and sales-loaded mutual funds to a predomi-
nant middle-class clientele.

Thus, the rhetorical question is, "How many of the advisor's clients
are driving six-figure European sports cars to a high-end restaurant on a
weekday evening?"

Any client experiencing such luxury is perhaps a fabulous thing.
Maybe a few of the sports car owner's clients are driving Toyotas or
Chevys and aspiring to such material gain by investing hard-earned dol-
lars with this money manager who presents an aura of wealth. Neverthe-

less, are the clients joining in the financial bliss by allocating investable dollars to the high fees and commissions generating products?

In the lopsided, 1-percent-owns-90-percent-of-the-wealth-economy, perhaps few indeed.

Build *Your* Vacation Home — Not Your Advisor's

It is customary for the do-it-yourself investor to overweight favorite publicly traded corporations in a portfolio. How does one know what companies will do better in the long run?

Although bordering on speculation, we can make an educated guess based on research and due diligence. Keeping conjecture to a minimum is perhaps the best approach to successful investing over the long term.

My experience and observations shared in this book whittle down to cultivating an equal-weighted basket of the common shares of quality companies purchased at bargain prices and held for an extended duration with the objective of a majority of the stocks outperforming the market. Nonetheless, why don't more investors follow the low-cost, equal-weighted, buy-and-hold, quality-purchased-at-a-value-price approach to portfolio construction?

Perhaps the purveyors of the Wall Street fee machine cannot build beach houses or drive sports cars on the minimal fees and commissions generated from the portfolio of the long-tailed, retail-level value investor. Instead, the Wall Street machine promotes and advocates bonus-generating advisory or investment fee models. Thus, institutional investors engage in options, short-selling, arbitrage, technical analysis, momentum investing, trend following, high-yield dividend, and other speculative, rampant turnover-driven trading platforms designed to underwrite pleasure drives to weekend retreats.

A more profitable alternative for the retail investor is to pursue the dream of building their own beach or lake house by taking a thoughtful, disciplined, and patient approach to portfolio construction, capital allocation, and dividend reinvestment.

Must You Ditch Your Money Manager?

The short answers are no and maybe.

This book is impartial to the firing of your investment advisor, financial planner, or broker, whether operating on Wall Street or Main Street. Many reputable, fee-only advisors or planners, as well as ethical discount brokers, exist and have the best interests of their clients at heart. Plus, laws and regulations hold registered investment advisors to a fiduciary responsibility of always acting in their clients' best interests.

As implied with the sports car-driving financial planner, the advisory fees and broker commissions—more than the advisors—are the focus and ire of *Build Wealth with Common Stocks*. If you are paying more than 1 percent annualized in combined fees and commissions on your investments, you are paying too much. And 0.75 to 1 percent is on the high end of what is reasonable and possible.

If your advisor is charging you lower than 1 percent annualized—with zero commissioned products—and you are happy with the performance and service, by all means, stay the course. But if you are inundated with excessive fees unsupported by relative returns, as are many retail investors, contemplating the alternative is perhaps in order. When considering new or continued services of a financial advisor, decide with thought and contemplation as opposed to emotional reactions.

Moreover, if you are already a self-directed investor, focus your energy on keeping your portfolio fees and commissions as low as possible. Online discount brokers, low-cost mutual and exchange-traded fund companies, and, for passive investors, dividend reinvestment plans (DRIPS) are suitable places to start.

Part III: Chapter Eighteen provides a narrative on controlling portfolio costs.

Sophisticated Research Scores Bonuses

There are no extra points for complex or deep-dive research other than perhaps bonus-generating fees produced by the Wall Street professional's dutiful exercise in intellectual prowess. The skeptical individual investor on Main Street asks, "What about portfolio performance from the investment thesis?"

If the complicated sell-side and buy-side research produced consistent market-beating outcomes, don't we become wealthy by following the published investment calls?

Based on the historical results, the answer is more no than yes. The Wall Street machine has convinced the masses that sophisticated approaches to research are the best paths to making money from investing. As it turns out, the fees collected as a derivative of the analysis generate a significant share of the profits by an institutional advisor or content provider.

Listen to quarterly earnings conference calls, dismissing the numbers-crunching or forecasts as the crystal ball-wielding prognosticators release plenty of bold predictions, pre- and post-call in the accompanying releases. Instead, listen closely to how senior management delivered the reported earnings than to what the team is guiding in the customary act of gaming analysts' estimates. Obtain better reads of senior management's confidence and conviction by taking note of the context of the call instead of the content of the results and the guidance.

For the benefit of your portfolio, have the courage and conviction to filter the noise of Wall Street.

* * *

CHAPTER TWO SUMMARY

On Demystifying Wall Street

- Bonus-generating fees notwithstanding, the investor on Main Street with limited capital has the potential to achieve superior returns with lower costs and less risk than a power broker working on Wall Street.

- The more profitable approach to retail investing is putting quality before speculation.

- Target a total-return horizon with a slow and steady long-view, counter to the get-rich-quick mentality of the day trader, trend follower, or momentum investor.

- If mulling new or continued services of a financial advisor, decide with thought, discussion, and contemplation as opposed to emotional reactions.

- Unlike the movies, there are no scripted endings or guaranteed outcomes in investing.

Three

Compound With A Margin of Safety

As an active, noninstitutional investor, be aware of the risks of investing in the stocks and bonds of publicly traded companies. Keep on guard against sudden market exuberance for candidates—Bitcoin and tech stocks were the latest flavors of choice—queued to take down an entire market. Unpredictable macroeconomic events such as the COVID-19 coronavirus pandemic are the exception.

Remember junk bonds in the 1980s, dot-coms in the 1990s, and mortgage-backed securities in the 2000s?

Between bubbles, irrational investor sentiment from the daily news cycle and quarterly earnings releases provoke gyrations within the US domestic stock market. The volatility keeps your holdings on a roller coaster ride in the short term as you wait for the compounded capital and income growth of your portfolio in the long term. Mitigate those risks by employing a value-based, long-view common stock portfolio strategy. Hold the shares for as long as the business remains terrific, as demonstrated by growing revenues and earnings, and, most important, by generating free cash flow and capital allocations that produce compounding annual returns for you, the shareholder.

Just as crucial as compounding is having wide margins of safety built into the common stocks of your chosen publicly traded companies.

The Magic of Compounding

Compounding is the financial process when an investor reinvests the owners' earnings, such as capital gains, interest payments, or dividend payouts back into the asset or portfolio with the intent of spawning additional profits from the holdings over time. This magical principle of mathematics is the primary generator of real returns from equity and fixed-income investing.

An Apple a Day

Apple (AAPL) went public on December 12, 1980, at $22 per share. The stock had split five times since the initial public offering (IPO), splitting on a two-for-one basis on June 16, 1987, June 21, 2000, and February 28, 2005. The stock split on a seven-for-one basis on June 9, 2014, and on a four-for-one basis on August 31, 2020.[1] A stock split occurs when a company divides its existing ordinary shares into multiples, adjusting the traded price by the same division. For example, if one share trading at $40 splits two for one, the result is two shares trading at $20.

On a split-adjusted basis, Apple's IPO share price was a mere ten cents after adjusting the cost from the original $22. As a bonus, the company paid quarterly dividends from April 1987 to October 1995 and again from July 2012. The result was a $1,000 investment during the IPO in December 1980, adjusted for stock splits and dividends, was worth about $3.5 million—accounting for inflation in 2020 dollars—as of the date of this calculation when the stock was trading at $113 a share.

Apple's captivating story of the power of compounded buy-and-hold investing reminds the retail-level investor to forge a commitment to total return from capital appreciation and dividend payments. And, as of this writing, Apple was the largest reported holding in Warren Buffett's Berkshire Hathaway portfolio.

It's the Real Thing for Real Investors

Upon its IPO on September 5, 1919, one common share of Coca-Cola (KO) traded at $40 a share—not adjusted for inflation—about the same price range during the research and writing of this book. Nevertheless, as of the split in July 2012, the estate of an original buy-and-hold purchaser has enjoyed eleven varied stock splits yielding 9,216 shares from the lone original share.[2] At the time of this calculation, the total value of the original single share equates to $5.5 million—accounting for inflation in 2020 dollars—net of dividends.

Thus, based on the share price of $50 as of this writing, a $200 investment in KO in 1919 was worth about $34.5 million—accounting for inflation in 2020 dollars—as of this calculation, net of dividends. The storied history of Coke is another prime example of why the retail investor cherishes the power of annual compounding from buying and holding the shares of wonderful companies that enjoy enduring competitive advantages from in-demand products or services.

> *The ideal business is one that earns very high returns on capital, and that keeps using lots of capital at those high returns. That becomes a compounding machine.*[3]
>
> —WARREN BUFFETT

In his answer to a shareholder question, Buffett—the eminent investor of our time—rendered wisdom in advocating the buying and holding of common shares of quality companies with the history and continued likelihood of generating high capital returns to grow the business. In turn, compounding total return from capital gains and dividends rewards the shareholder. Coca-Cola—a favorite long-term holding of Buffett's Berkshire Hathaway—has been a compounding machine for a century.

There are investors, and there are speculators. Each seeks to profit, the former in the long term and the latter in the short term. The long-view investor seems to prevail thanks to the magic of compounding.

Protected By a Wide Margin of Safety

Compounding capital gains and dividends are the best friends of the common stock investor. Buffett's mentor Benjamin Graham, in his classic book *The Intelligent Investor*,[4] speaks of limiting stock purchases to shares trading with a *margin of safety*.

Margin of Safety in Practice

The margin of safety in a stock is the difference between the estimated intrinsic value of the security and its actual market price. In general, an investor has two options to calculate the margin of safety in a company and its common shares. The conventional approach attempts to predict an exact intrinsic value of the equity and then subtracts the estimate from the actual price. The second, more practical method uncovers whether the stock represents a quality, enduring company trading at what appears to be a reasonable price. The former requires high intelligence and plenty of assumptions; the latter presents mere thought and discipline in a review of the facts.

Some well-intentioned investors prefer to calculate the margin of safety with discounted future free cash flow projections and other future-focused or assumptive estimates of precision price targets cast within specific time frames. Wall Street analysts enable the behavior on Main Street by publishing complex financial models that lack consistency. These sophisticated margin of safety or intrinsic value estimates are what justifies the high fee structure of Wall Street. Be suspect of the projections within these formulas. Hasn't an investor who starts predicting future cash flows, interest rates, and capital expenditures become more of a speculator?

Nearsighted predictions are more or less crapshoots, yet Wall Street makes a living off of them, a paradox of epic proportions.

Margin of Safety by Proxy

Interpret the useful measure of the intrinsic worth of a company and its stock based on current and trailing indices as opposed to assumptive discounted future cash flows and other cross-your-fingers projections. Attempt a modest, albeit realistic, approach to estimating inherent value by measuring the margin of safety in a broader sense.

Part II: Strategies offers conservative models to screen for the bargain-priced shares of companies with strong value propositions, favorable earnings and free cash flow yields—as compared to the Ten-Year Treasury rate—adequate returns on equity and invested capital; attractive prices to sales, operating cash flow, and enterprise value to operating earnings; and controllable long- and short-term debt coverage.

When a company and its common shares present as superior in each margin of safety indicator, a higher potential for market-beating performance exists. Quantify the performance of the operation in more objective than subjective terms. No-brainers are better bets than possiblys or maybes.

Instead of chasing the dragon, own common shares to savor the benefit of partnering with a company supporting its customers with in-demand, useful products or services, rewarding employees with sustainable career opportunities, and compensating shareholders with positive returns protected by world-class internal financial controls.

The thoughtful, do-it-yourself investor avoids attempts at predicting specific future movements in the shares, whether by price target or percentage gains and losses, leaving nonsensical games of chance to market speculators. Nonetheless, the historical capital gains in the common shares spawn from the occasional, sometimes generous, upticks in the stock price of a high-quality business adding up over time. It is the patient investor who experiences this alpha or the excess return of an investment relative to the performance of a benchmark index.

Any ongoing dividend yields are the stock market equivalent of receiving interest payments on the outstanding principal of a loan or the equivalent of the initial capital investment to purchase the shares of the stock.

On *Becoming Warren Buffett*

My investment objective enthusiastically follows the rational wisdom of the Oracle of Omaha. As presented in the excellent HBO documentary *Becoming Warren Buffett,*[5] Buffett bought cheap companies earlier in his career, regardless of quality, and unlocked value through corporate events by dumping the stock when the price increased to a predetermined level. He then transitioned to buying and holding quality companies at sensible prices and taking advantage of the magic of compounding protected by a wide margin of safety.

Buffett acknowledges that it was under the tutelage of his partner, Charlie Munger when he made this career makeover from a stock trader to a company investor. He learned from Munger that "it is far better to buy a wonderful business at a fair price than a fair business at a wonderful price."

If modeling Buffett's earlier career, the cautious advice reminds the stock trader to sell a fair company at a fantastic price or live with the consequences. On the contrary, if influenced by the Buffett/Munger partnership that resolved to buy and hold terrific companies at fair prices, the independent investor is better served staying for the long haul, as this was the holding period when Buffett's fortune began to compound into the billions. Nevertheless, his valuable lesson and the basis of the documentary — what a successful investor does with a portfolio windfall is far more important than the act of making money. Buffett is giving a bulk of his wealth back to society through charities such as the Bill and Melinda Gates Foundation.

The HBO documentary presents a profound juxtaposition of Buffett's eccentric accumulation of enormous wealth against his ultimate decision to divest a majority of his investable assets to philanthropic causes, including those presided by his children. My takeaways were:

you cannot go wrong, financially, by modeling his greedy, albeit compassed ways; intellectually, from his mountains of wisdom; and spiritually, by giving it back when the scoreboard reads Game Over. Hence, a stark reminder that one cannot take a lifelong accumulation of tangible assets to any Promised Land or afterlife.

Capital notwithstanding, the thoughtful investor who follows Buffett's time-tested paradigm of taking advantage of the magic of compounding protected by a wide margin of safety increases the likelihood of success over a long-term holding period.

Build and Maintain Wealth with Common Stocks

During the research and writing of this book, the overextended post-Great Recession bull market, including the unpredictable gyrations forced by the irrational sentiment of traders and speculators, was another reminder to stay invested in the common shares of quality companies. By doing so, you take advantage of the compounding capital gains and dividends protected by wide margins of safety.

As it went, the exuberance reversed in a heartbeat from the coronavirus pandemic.

When searching for bargains to add to your portfolio during a bull market and finding that new opportunities are nonexistent at the moment, you are better off just staying put. Remember, the good ideas already sitting in your portfolio are often the best opportunities to allocate dry powder—investable cash insured by the Federal Deposit Insurance Corporation or FDIC—as opposed to investing in speculative or desperate new ideas. Believing the historic post-Great Recession business cycle was somehow different, investors were chasing visions of fast money from waves on technical charts and other speculative fads of the moment. The penchant of the herd for irrational behavior was in full gear. And then COVID-19 became the number one story with a bullet.

The pursuit of alpha equates to a portfolio of dividend-paying common stocks of quality companies outperforming the corresponding benchmark over time, plus exceeding any other expectations of the disciplined, long-view investor. Notwithstanding any attractive buying or profit-taking opportunities, current market cycles—whether bull, bear, or range-bound*—are irrelevant in the scheme of buy-and-hold investing.

Within the perpetual uncertainty of economic cycles, it is crucial to evaluate downside risk and other measurements of the margin of safety of the stock in the near view to take advantage of the compounding of the capital gains and dividends in the longer view.

* * *

*Bull: an economy that is growing and the broader market is on the rise. Bear: an economy that is receding and most stocks are declining in value. Range-bound: prices are constrained and lie between certain upper and lower limits.

* * *

CHAPTER THREE SUMMARY

On Compounding with a Margin of Safety

- Buy and hold the stocks of quality companies with the history—and continued likelihood—of compounding total return from capital gains and dividends across every market cycle.

- Since volatile markets are perpetual, it is crucial to evaluate the downside risk and other measurements of the margin of safety in a stock price, a concept originated by the father of value investing Benjamin Graham.

■ In the spirit of the shared wisdom of Warren Buffet and Charlie Munger, the thoughtful retail investor buys slices of terrific companies at fair prices as opposed to fair companies at terrific prices.

■ What a successful investor does with a portfolio windfall is far more important than the act of making that money.

■ Live well within your means.

Four

Apply Common Sense

To paraphrase American baseball legend Yogi Berra, investing is '90 percent half' common sense. 'The other half' is patience and discipline. As much as the institutional way of stock-picking attempts to convince you otherwise, it is far from rocket science.

Keep investing super simple, and the beneficiaries of your portfolio will thank you. And when the Wall Street fee machine insists that its complex investing paradigms are best, remember that keeping it simple with a pinch of common sense are primary tenets of successful, do-it-yourself portfolio management.

Discover Your Circle of Competence

Be committed to a thoughtful approach to longer-view value investing. The mantra includes understanding and accepting the limitations of your circle of competence as you avoid the crowd's bias toward expensive investments. Have you ever noticed that institutional investors tend to favor financials at higher proportions than other sectors?

It is because each exists as a full-time member of the financial services industry, and the sector presents as an investment comfort zone by default. Whether professional or independent, the investor develops a sphere of competence that defines one's success in specific market niches.

My circle of competence—developed from over twenty years of retail-level investing—is limited to six sectors: communications services, consumer discretionary, consumer staples, health care, industrials, and technology.

- The new communications services sector was spun off from the consumer discretionary and the former telecommunications sectors and includes an original holding in our family portfolio: The Walt Disney Company (DIS).

- Consumer discretionary companies consist of easy-to-understand products and services, although at higher risk because cyclical stocks dominate the sector.

- The consumer staples sector also covers easy-to-understand products or services and, as noncyclical businesses, at a lower risk.

- Health care is perhaps to the twenty-first century America what the automobile industry was to the twentieth century: the centerpiece of the domestic economy.

- Industrials are manufacturing things an everyday investor understands for the most part.

- It is sometimes challenging to comprehend the products and services of technology companies; however, the value propositions are often compelling.

By default, I am in contempt of the other five sectors. Here is why I avoid each:

- Financials — often too leveraged and overinvested by Wall Street.

- Real estate or real estate investment trusts (REITs) because a significant portion of our family's net worth is home equity. Only if a renter or retiree would I include quality REITs in the portfolio.

- Energy stocks tend to go up and down with energy prices more than the performance of the representative companies.

- Materials are volatile, commodity-based stocks. See energy above.

- Utilities are overregulated and often indebted, although perhaps a wise choice for retirees seeking income diversification.

Staying within your circle of competence is a sage method to help protect your principal. What sectors or industries are in your sphere of competency?

Avoid the Crowd

History dictates the retail portfolio of the investor who follows the crowd—whether the favorite momentum stocks of fellow retail investors or the Wall Street flavor of the month—will often lose momentum at market extremes. The COVID-19 coronavirus pandemic was a vivid example of this stock market phenomenon.

Following some self-reflection, I concluded that market-cap-weighting our family portfolio was akin to following the investor crowd. Higher market capitalizations—defined as shares outstanding times the stock price—signal the market has perhaps overbought the stock.

Some time ago, I changed the structure of The Model Portfolio to equal-weight; thus, each of the holdings in the portfolio represents an identical percentage of the total portfolio as opposed to a weighted share arrangement based on market capitalization. Hence, the overall performance since inception lowered a bit after rebalancing from market-weight to equal-weight. Nonetheless, the individual performance and weighing against the benchmark, based on the date of inclusion in the portfolio, remained constant.

My intent for tracking the cumulative portfolio performance has always centered on presenting individual holdings and overall portfolio outcomes in a simple format to test the investing strategies. The equal-weight methodology continues this tradition for readers and members.

The proven way to make money in the market long-term is staying invested for the unpredictable, albeit welcomed price jumps, cultivating a portfolio that is less vulnerable to sudden and unexpected price drops such as was triggered by the coronavirus pandemic. To accomplish this feat, unlike many in the crowd, you must have the courage to stay invested through each market cycle.

My Journey as a Common Stock Investor

I became a bottom-up value investor from trial and error after failing at top-down macro research earlier in my self-managed retail investing career. At some level, I have tried many of the genres defining the stock market: momentum growth, trend following, technical analysis, sector investing, fund strategies, and similar macroeconomic approaches to portfolio construction.

I learned a hard lesson in retail investing from this high-cost investment education — I paid tuition in the form of trading losses. Luckily for me, the trial-and-error experiences kept bringing me back to the concept of value.

Longer-view value investing has an enduring legacy, including the inevitable ups and downs, similar to every other experience in the stock market and in our lives. When executed with a value bent, do-it-yourself investing leaves us less vulnerable to the traps that sometimes compromise the Wall Street professional manager. These practices include forced quarterly portfolio activities to protect job security, satisfying the institutional or accredited investor's thirst for fast money, and charging bloated fees to bankroll bonuses.

I am humbled and proud the investment principle of common sense has continued to work well for our family and for dedicated readers and listeners, above and beyond the pre-coronavirus thousand-legged bull market occurring at the time of researching this book.

Since its inception—as the Great Recession became the second-worst economic downtown in American history—the holdings of The Model Portfolio enjoyed a cumulative average capital return that had outperformed the S&P 500. These results (available at davidjwaldron.com) were as of June 30, 2020, quarter-end close, adjusted for splits and dividends, and based on an equal cap-weighted basis. As further discussed in Chapter Ten, although *price* is what I paid for ownership slices of these excellent companies, *value*, over time, is what I got.

The market-beating outcome took over ten years of diligent—albeit enjoyable—work, and there is no guarantee the outperformance continues. Building wealth from a self-managed investment portfolio over an extended holding period is rare compared to professional managers collecting millions of dollars in portfolio fees each quarter.

John Bogle Meets Warren Buffett

Respect the low-cost, lesser-risk foundation of index investing promoted passionately for decades by the late Vanguard Group founder John Bogle. Aspire to the gratification and potential rewards of Warren Buffett-style active investing, albeit with minimal capital. Despite compromising some of the lesser risks of passive investing, the do-it-yourself investor who enjoys researching and owning businesses through common stocks still delights in active investing and at a lower cost.

Acknowledging that I was leaving too much money on the table in the form of 1 to 2 percent annual investment advisory fees, the collective wisdom of Buffett and Bogle grabbed my attention. Discover how to invest with the discipline and patience of Buffett and at the lower costs and lesser risk advocated by Bogle.

In other words, add a pinch of common sense.

The Wall Street Consensus is Often Senseless

As an individual investor on Main Street, avoid interpreting the Wall Street consensus as a definitive buy or sell signal, and instead, as perhaps a suggestion to move in the other direction. During celebrated quarterly earnings seasons, after a company comes up short on analyst consensus estimates of earnings or revenue, ask who missed: the senior management of the enterprise or the Wall Street analysts?

Emotional investing seems to produce losses more often than gains. Emotional intelligence (EQ), on the other hand, is more critical to investing success than the intelligence quotient (IQ). Thus, the thoughtful Main Street investor has the temperament to outperform the high IQ Ivy Leaguer of Wall Street. Regardless, combine a high IQ with an elevated EQ, and you're looking at a super investor. Bogle and Buffett come to mind again, as does Benjamin Graham, Seth Klarman, Peter Lynch, and Howard Marks, among other high-profile value investors.

Many investors—for better, although more often for worse—trade on geopolitical news and other macroeconomic events, inspiring passionate feelings more than emotional intellect. On the contrary, the long-only, buy-and-hold-forever investor on Main Street practices discipline to endure the peaks and valleys of the volatile journey of common stocks in the short-term trading vacuum called Wall Street.

By using common sense, the thoughtful investor knows that quarterly earnings, news, and other short-term events create buying opportunities for the common stocks of already determined quality enterprises. In contrast, countless investors sell at a loss on the report or event by placing emotion before intellect.

Take a Rearview and Side View Focus

Although the life lessons of hindsight also apply to investing, foresight, or predicting the direction of the market and stock prices with consistency, is implausible. As such, my research and ensuing theses of targeted common stocks tend to be rearview and side view focused. This driving investment philosophy implies the rearview mirror representing the past, and the side view mirror indicating the present are each clear; however, the windshield projecting the future is foggy.

As underscored throughout the book, I place minimal weight on the forward consensus. It is every bit speculative to me; thus, the foggy windshield. Many active investors—whether professional or individual—underperform the market over time. Each is buying or selling based on speculation of what is going to happen in the future via price targets, earnings estimates, sales volume, potential mergers and acquisitions, or market corrections. Despite conveying confidence, does any forecaster know what is going to happen to a market, company, or stock price at any specific time in the future?

I don't and refuse to pretend at your expense or the account balances in my family's portfolio. For example, if a targeted stock is down 3 percent the day after initiating a position, the stock trader is second-guessing the decision against waiting one more day to buy. The thoughtful investor, who purchased the same stock at $50, is waiting with patience for a split-adjusted $500 a share years down the road. In contrast, the market-timing trader is buying at $48 the next day and selling at $53—or worse, $43—after the next earnings release.

Investing based on predicting future events is no different from investing based on hope. Predictive investment analysis is nothing more than hopefulness disguised as intelligent forecasting. I weather occasional heat—pun intended—from readers and editors of my research for focusing more on the actual makeup of the company and the valuation of the stock price and less on the forward predictions of where the products, markets, and customers are heading.

I am in this game to buy and hold the common stocks of quality enterprises, as opposed to providing entertainment value for the whims of readers. Again, leave the Magic 8-Ball part of the investment thesis to Wall Street analysts and senior management. Analysts make more money from fees—and management from stock options—than from compounded annual growth in capital gains and dividends as we do on Main Street.

It seems just yesterday the movie rental store Blockbuster Video was propped up by the investment community based on forecasted global store growth in renting its DVDs. The internet was upon us, and the bulls were predicting Blockbuster conquering that as well. Those who studied the company and its stock price knew it was far from a good buy based on limited barriers to entry and other issues at the time. And the bears won out based on that approach to investing. The investment thesis is more often right there in front of us, negating the need to take a risky trip down some murky road of predictive analysis.

By limiting stock purchases to excellent businesses selling at affordable share prices, the future takes care of itself. Invest based on objective facts, ducking the ever-present subjective forecasts. That has worked for me since I reinvented my approach to investing over ten years ago, including during the 2008–2009 financial crisis and the coronavirus pandemic in 2020. Being that I am neither a stock guru nor a market wunderkind, I am confident the approach works just as well for the motivated reader.

In time, the thoughtful retail investor learns the Yogism of the financial markets where investing is 90 percent half common sense. The other half, up next in Chapter Five, is patience and discipline.

* * *

CHAPTER FOUR SUMMARY

On Common Sense Investing

- Discover your circle of competence in the sectors and industries that house the common shares of your targeted companies.

■ History dictates the retail portfolio of the investor following the crowd often loses momentum at market extremes. Sidestep the herd.

■ The Wall Street consensus is often senseless. Avoid the temptation to interpret the accord as a definitive buy or sell signal and, instead, as a suggestion to perhaps run the other way.

■ Buying and selling common stocks based on predicting a future event is no different from investing based on hope. Stick to the objective facts and ignore the subjective forecasts.

■ To paraphrase baseball legend Yogi Berra, investing is 90 percent half common sense. The other half—up next in Chapter Five—is patience and discipline.

Five

Practice Patience And Discipline

Patience is perhaps the scarcest—and thereby, the most valuable—commodity on Wall Street. The individual investor on Main Street gets to profit from this market incongruity.

The patient common stock investor knows if they wait long enough, their targeted quality companies—including some already in their portfolio and now trading at higher valuations since initial purchase—become available at bargain prices, if only temporarily. Consequently, investors or traders who lack patience often pay more for the equities purchased. Why pay more?

And the disciplined investor forever places the fear of losing money over the fear of missing out.

Wait for the Batting Practice Pitch Before Swinging

A surprise macro occurrence, controllable company event, a market downturn, a negative news report, or a quarterly earnings miss often trigger buying opportunities of excellent companies for the patient value investor as opposed to panic selling in lockstep with the herd. Thus, it is in our best interest to maintain a separate watchlist or wishlist containing the ticker symbols of companies to consider owning for the compounding returns over the long-term when the price is right. Wait patiently for the market to throw you a batting practice pitch by lowering the price of a targeted stock because of the fleeting, shortsighted reasoning of the crowd.

Being a scarce and thereby valuable commodity on Wall Street, embracing patience is often the difference between success and failure as an investor. Despite the imposing challenge, practicing patience in waiting for your investment theses to play out is paramount to long-term success. Contrary to conventional wisdom, it is rare to create wealth in financial markets from short-term trading; however, perseverance is often rewarded.

The disciplined investor pursues alpha by researching companies with sound fundamentals trading at sensible valuations and demonstrating the propensity for upside, in addition to exhibiting downside protection or a margin of safety of the invested capital. Then, if choosing to purchase, wades with patience through market and company gyrations for the thesis on the stock to play out over a long-term holding period.

Investor patience changes the conversation from the proverbial Wall Street way of quarter-to-quarter reactions to revenue or earnings hits and misses to the intelligent investor model of multiyear compounding returns on capital and dividends purchased at value prices.

Hindsight is 20/20; patience is always forward.

Be Disciplined to Buy and Hold Forever

I equate the premise of buy-and-hold-forever as a commitment to companies—and the common stocks representing each—to buy low, hold high, sell when you die. Be willing to hold the common shares of great companies for a generation, enjoying the compounding growth of capital and dividends. Sell when you die translates to passing the asset on to your heirs or designated charities, as the information thus far is vague on whether stocks are trading in any afterlife.

The challenge for many investors is to think ten to twenty years out as opposed to ten to twenty months or even ten to twenty days. Imagine you are a partner in a successful private business with a terrific product line, ubiquitous brand name, and double-digit net margins and returns on capital. The CFO announces the gross margin has dropped from 43 to 42 percent because of an unforeseen currency exchange issue and is forecasted to level off at 40 percent by next year. Do you storm into a partners' meeting demanding permission to sell your shares as if a market trader?

Ever present, the Wall Street reaction to earnings oscillates between exuberance and panic. Stock prices and valuations go up and down with the mania of a roller coaster. The welcome news is the creation of outstanding buying opportunities. From there, the gains seem to creep up over time for the patient and disciplined investor on Main Street.

The Voting Machine vs. the Weighing Machine

> *As Ben (Graham) said: "In the short-run, the market is a voting machine, but in the long run it is a weighing machine."[1]*
> —WARREN BUFFETT

Wall Street is notorious for demanding steady, quarter-to-quarter growth in sales and profits, with the market pounding any stock missing company guidance or analysts' forecasts. Warren Buffett's words that open this section recalls the teachings of Benjamin Graham during the notorious struggles of the stock market in the 1930s, and it still holds today, whether bull or bear market.

Per Buffett, Graham meant that in the near view, investors and traders vote for stocks based on popularity and sizzle, anticipating the performance of the stock when hitting or missing its quarterly projections, for instance. He reasoned that stock voters often pay a premium when following the crowd. In contrast, the patient and disciplined value investor weighs the stock's worthiness and whether the price is appealing. Buy or sell a stock based on its inherent value from the weighing machine as opposed to its perceived value from the voting machine.

Buffett and Graham's shared theory is the equivalent of having the market serve you instead of you serving the market, as do many investors. As day traders or momentum investors cast votes daily, the disciplined investor weighs carefully the fundamental analysis of a company tempered by the patience to act only when the stock price is attractive. Look for a business with a long history of slow or moderate growth, offering a sustainable value proposition to its customers, coupled with steady returns for the shareholders.

Patience—the rarest commodity on Wall Street and Main Street—combined with discipline outlast the trivial ways investors tend to manage portfolios with impatience and ignorance, thus making the most precious commodities on Wall Street your best friends.

The Disciplined Investor Seldom Loses Money

A primary tenet of profitable, do-it-yourself investing is the discipline never to lose money. A simple rule dictates that an investor cannot lose money unless selling out the position after it declines below the cost basis. Universal to value-based common stock investing, this concept distinguishes the ever-present dichotomy of realized and unrealized gains in our portfolios. Dividend payouts notwithstanding, an investor loses money on a stock when selling shares for a realized loss as opposed to waiting patiently for a realized gain.

Indeed, the inverse is true, as the capital gains of individually held stocks are treated as unrealized or paper profits until the investor executes and settles a trade. Nevertheless, unrealized paper gains are always more fun, and paper losses are more palatable than realized losses.

Market history dictates the crowd is often wrong. When a stock or an entire market drops 20 percent in one day, investors often panic and sell at a loss. I have read investment reports, articles, and comments from portfolio managers, financial authors, or investors who disclose selling shares of a tanking stock. The writer sometimes hides behind the theory of sunk cost or unrecoverable money already spent. Nonetheless, selling out the stock below the cost basis guarantees the original capital invested is forever lost. The speculative trader sells now with the emotional cover of the sunk cost theory; the patient investor sells later at a profit above the cost basis.

Most important is the preservation of the principal capital invested. The thoughtful, independent investor remains prosperous by pledging never to lose money. Successful investors practice discipline in every approach to the investment paradigm.

Repel the Greatest Fear of the Retail Investor

The primary fear of many investors is not a market crash.

During the time of researching and writing this book, a bull market for the record books—where illusions of fast money proliferated even as bargains became scarce—tested the thoughtfulness, discipline, and patience of the value-based investor. Then, COVID-19 crashed the party.

In any upmarket cycle, those who compromise and join the herd in scooping up overpriced growth stocks, poor-quality value traps, or tempting fads because of the fear of missing out (FOMO) regret their purchases when the market retreats as it did when the coronavirus pandemic hit. Thus, here is a question for the do-it-yourself investor to ask at the pinnacle of a bull market: "What do I dread the most, the fear of missing out or the fear of losing money?"

A portfolio built on the fear of losing money has more potential to outperform the market over a long-term horizon than a basket of trades constructed on fads or trends purchased on the fear of missing out. As a bonus, the partial ownership of superior companies gives the thoughtful, disciplined, and patient investor the sense of contributing to socioeconomic opportunities for loved ones, their country, and the world.

The Baby Elephant on the Trading Floor

It is wise to address the baby elephant in the room by taking a look at the history of corrections and bear markets. It is never as bad as the headlines or frenzied trading activity make it out to be. Depending on the economic cycle, ask: Are we in a correction—defined as a broad market index, such as the Dow Jones Industrials, S&P 500, or NASDAQ-100, being down more than 10 percent from its market high—or are we experiencing an extended bear market?

Whether entering a prolonged bear market—such as 20 percent off the highs—or experiencing the so-called bull market head fake, it is essential to remind the retail-level investor that each market direction is an opportunity.

- Market correction: bargain-hunting time for quality names at reasonable prices; however, resist selling underperformers at a loss, if at all possible.

- Sustained bull market: continue to grow your portfolio with the magic of compounding as you prune your long-term holdings, if warranted, for profit-taking or rebalancing from any recent overheating.

- Sustained bear market: buy, buy, and buy as the crowd screams bye, bye, and bye.

The disciplined and patient investor will sell or reduce holdings only at a profit.

A History of S&P 500 Corrections

Taking a closer look at S&P 500 corrections illustrates the opportunity presented during emotion-testing times for investors.

According to a January 2018 report from Goldman Sachs's chief global equity strategist Peter Oppenheimer,[2] throughout market history, S&P 500 corrections and bear markets have durations of between one and thirty-one months. And just nine of the thirty-seven corrections lasted longer than twelve months. Recoveries often have lengthier durations, although perhaps each is more profitable than the corresponding correction.

The study showed how bull market corrections averaged a drop of 13 percent over four months and took about the same length of time to recover. When the S&P fell at least 20 percent from its record high into the bear market territory, the pain lasted for twenty-two months on average. The typical decline was 30 percent for bear markets.

A takeaway from Oppenheimer's study is the best-practices approach to corrections or bear markets is the self-reminder that we are far from the end of the world as we know it. An intriguing portfolio opportunity is perhaps at our fingertips more than any ensuing, albeit short-lived havoc from the downturn. Nevertheless, at the time of writing this chapter, fate was pending on whether the coronavirus pandemic was driving a hoped-for brief market correction in the context of a controlled outbreak, or worse, a sustained bear market as the dire consequence of human suffering from health or economic distress.

The Formula for Stock Market Investing Success

As far as sudden, volatile, and unpredictable markets, future downturns will come and go as the market forever remains unpredictable. You can bet this time and the next time are no different in the context of quality bargains once again abounding for the disciplined and patient investor flush with FDIC-insured cash. When will it happen again?

Despite the inevitable volatility, I have no idea and forever dismiss expert predictions on market trends, stock prices, and interest rate movements as no more dependable than the entertaining Ouija board. Remain steadfast in buying and holding the stocks of quality companies to outperform the roller coaster movements of the market over time. On the contrary, trading stocks and currencies on speculation in the quest for fast money is fleeting, and the house wins most of those wagers anyhow.

Instead of placing bets on speculative equities, start investing in wonderful companies trading at fair prices. There is no more superior investment strategy over the lifetime of an investor than embracing the concept of quality plus value, further leveraged by the productive fear of losing money, as opposed to a destructive fear of missing out.

The sum of thought plus discipline plus patience plus a pinch of common sense equals stock market investing success.

* * *

CHAPTER FIVE SUMMARY

On Patience, Discipline, and the Fear of Losing Money

- Patience is the scarcest and, thereby, the most valuable commodity available to the retail-level common stock investor.

- Investors or traders who lack discipline are apt to pay more for securities. Why pay more?

- Wait for the market to throw you a batting practice pitch representing a lowered price for a targeted stock because of the fleeting, shortsighted reasoning of the crowd.

- One rule guarantees you will almost never lose money on an investment: avoid selling shares below the cost basis.

- A portfolio built based on the fear of losing money is destined to outperform the market over a long-term horizon than if constructed on fads or trends purchased with the fear of missing out. Dodge the herd and its fear of missing out and focus on the fear of losing money. Your portfolio, and your loved ones, will thank you.

Six

Own Companies Instead Of
Trading Stocks

S top trading stocks and start investing in companies.
  The founding concept of buying and selling stocks facilitated willing participants to take affordable ownership slices of publicly traded companies. The original premise has evolved beyond the fundamentals-based ownership of common shares to a myriad of research methodologies, ownership classifications, and trading platforms. Seek companies with overall attractive long-term prospects, knowing the enduring quality of the operator remains paramount to the success of the investment over time.

This chapter addresses the intrinsic advantages of investing in quality companies at present value as opposed to placing bets on equities for speculative growth.

Trade a Cigar Butt or Invest in a Bottle of Wine

The so-called cigar butts and special situations—the common shares of fair companies available at cheap prices—are more about trading stocks and practicing arbitrage than investing in companies and are hence, speculative. On the other hand, equate the endurance of a quality enterprise to a long-lasting bottle of fine wine. The analogy is reminiscent of Warren Buffett's acknowledgment—as influenced by partner Charlie Munger—that he transformed from a stock trader to a company investor.

Munger's wisdom confirms that an investor who holds a concentrated basket of the common shares of high-quality companies and follows it with diligence has an increased potential to produce superior returns over the long term. On the contrary, trade in and out of stocks based on news, quarterly results, or market sentiment, and chances are, over an extended period, you will lose more often than win.

Get to Know the Business

Infamous stock picker, Peter Lynch, writes in his must-read book *Beating the Street,* "Behind every stock is a company. Find out what it's doing."[1] Lynch expresses a keen understanding of the distinction between the products or services of an enduring company as reflected in its earnings and the stock price.

I am neither smart nor foolish enough to time the market. Instead, I search for a margin of safety in five key quantitative and qualitative areas of the operational and equity performances of a targeted business, as further discussed in Part II: Strategies.

The successful, do-it-yourself investor targets profitable, cash-generating companies that are providing comfortable margins of safety. The disciplined investor owns companies with efficient and transparent management who leverage returns for customers, employees, and shareholders. Think of yourself as an investor who owns slices of excellent businesses instead of accumulating electronic shares of common stock purchased in an instant from your online discount broker. The actions are identical, perhaps, although the affirmation as an owner of companies is more substantial than being the trader of stocks.

After all, a bottle of fine wine lasts far longer than a cigar butt.

Avoid Speculative Growth: Invest in Present Value

> " *The choice isn't really between value and growth but between* "
> *value today and value tomorrow. Growth investing repre-*
> *sents a bet on company performance that may or may not*
> *materialize in the future, while value investing is based pri-*
> *marily on the analysis of a company's current wealth.*[2]
>
> —HOWARD MARKS

This section opens with an intelligent thought from the legendary value investor, money manager, and author Howard Marks from his essential book *The Most Important Thing*. The wisdom of Marks dictates a skeptical approach to modern methods of measurement used by momentum investors and day traders, such as technical analysis or the in-depth study of past price behavior. The defensive investor prefers companies already growing, discounting the customary promises of growth from analysts, financial bloggers, and senior management.

As Howard Marks does, focus on value investing in the fundamentals-driven analysis of equities. Value now often leads to growth later.

Value Begets Growth

When conducting due diligence for your portfolio, consider evaluating a minimum of three years of trailing growth in revenue, earnings per share, and dividend rates. Look for double-digit or at least favorable compound annual growth rates (CAGR). The potential for annualized compounding from total return on capital and dividends improves when purchasing common shares with wide margins of safety or at a price you believe is below your estimate of the intrinsic value of the representative underlying stock. Part II explores these strategies in depth.

With a nod of gratitude to the timeless wisdom of Howard Marks, avoid attempts at equity analysis that makes calls such as XYZ shares undervalued by 27 percent. The thoughtful, individual investor disavows any self-illusion of the ability to predict exact percentages of presumed pricing discrepancies, surmising from research and common sense that stocks only appear mispriced in general.

If such prognostication were more often right—being wrong the more frequent outcome—the so-called top 1 percent of wealth would grow closer to perhaps 50 percent of the population from buying and selling based on the magical price predictions. Until, of course, the zero-sum game of investing rears its head. Speculative growth stocks are apt to fall harder and faster in a down market than any rise in an upmarket. Nonetheless, in buying value now, an investor is better positioned to benefit from growth later.

Become an Informed Investor

I learned many lessons in personal investing. Looking back, I started as an uninformed investor who used a top-down macroeconomic approach to investing. I was ignorant of the style of investing that I followed at the time. In fairness, there are some successful top-down, macro-focused investors. My futile approach was forecasting the trends and buying baskets of stocks or funds that spoke to those perceived developments, whether information technology, biotechnology, or buying one stock from each sector of the S&P 500 and calling it a diversified index. You name it — I tried it and failed, although, in hindsight, each trade seemed a good idea at the time.

When I invested in a 401(k) at work, the typical choices were limited to a select basket of mutual funds with higher than average advisory fees. I was fortunate those funds included Charles Royce's Royce Total Return (RYTRX), William H. Browne's Tweedy, Browne Global Value (TBGVX), and the late Martin Whitman's Third Avenue Value (TVFVX). I read each quarterly and annual report from these seasoned, professional value investors, learning about bottom-up investing, the positive influence of Benjamin Graham, and how owning companies through disciplined investment was more noble and profitable than trading stocks on speculation.

Despite the excellent capital gains and dividends earned—as well as the acquired wisdom—I sold out each fund after the realization I was leaving too much money on the table in the form of investment advisory fees exceeding 1 percent per annum. At the same time, Warren Buffett, Peter Lynch, John Bogle, and Howard Marks were each capturing my attention. I learned it was possible to invest in publicly traded companies with the wisdom of Buffett, the stock-picking discipline of Lynch, at a lower cost as preached by Bogle, and with an understanding of the risk as advocated by Marks. Nevertheless, I am forever grateful to Chuck, Bill, and Marty for teaching me the art and science of value investing from afar. From the narratives of these gentlemen, I also learned the importance of writing an investment thesis with intermittent doses of wit, humor, and sarcasm. After all, it is just money.

In the short term, the crowd is almost always wrong. Trend investing is comparable to investing in junk bonds, the Slinky, or Bitcoin: a few make out big, although many lose big. "I'm gonna get in early and rake," says the uninformed investor.

The more worthy alternative is to outperform the market by becoming an informed investor.

Ignore the Wall Street Darlings

The thoughtful investor on Main Street knows that a stock coveted by Wall Street carries nominal weight as far as gauging the potential of the company or the intrinsic value of its stock price. I have worked for companies branded as Wall Street darlings and wondered if the analysts knew what I knew. And Wall Street ended up wrong each time. As high-flying start-ups, growth stocks sometimes are calculated bets worth taking; however, as long-term quality investments, each is more roll-of-the-dice or speculative at best. An exception to the rule is an enterprise whose name mirrors a particular fruit with a solid core and a reputation for keeping the doctor away.

Just think of those who bought $1,000 of Apple stock for a split-adjusted ten cents a share in 1980 yet bailed because of a perceived material issue. The rare shareholder who stuck with the stock for the return of Steve Jobs, the introductions of the iMac, iPod, iPhone, and iPad, plus the enduring leadership of Jobs' handpicked successor, Tim Cook, was rewarded handsomely, earning close to $3.5 million in capital gains when adjusted for reinvested dividends and inflation as of the calculation date. Apple presents a valid historical example of the buy-and-hold-forever method paying off for the patient investor.

Chasing Growth from A to Z

Elude the prediction game of specific future margins and cash flows, and instead find superb companies trading at reasonable prices from diligent research and analysis of the present value. Remember, in the stock-picking vehicle of the thoughtful, disciplined, and patient investor, the rearview and side view mirrors are clear, and the windshield is foggy. Invest with due diligence based on looking in the rear and side views and deploying common sense and instinct as opposed to looking forward through the windshield or into a crystal ball. Is this a company you'd invest in if owned as a private enterprise by a friend who asked you to become a partner?

Analysts and executives offer us projections and guidance. From there, the crowd attempts to estimate—or accept at face value—future earnings, stock price targets, margins, and cash flow. Yet, how reliable is the forecasted data?

Based on personal experience and observations, such prognostications are worthless. As an alternative, deduce from sound research the likelihood of the business continuing to produce or improve top-line revenue, profit margins, and free cash flow, in a general sense. Buy small stakes in excellent companies when macro or microeconomic events produce windows of value pricing opportunities. Avoid predictions of the precise direction of the stock price. As with other big-ticket items purchased during a lifetime, *caveat emptor* applies to common stock investing as well.

Hindsight being the proverbial 20/20, I missed the early fortunes of the online retail behemoth Amazon (NASDAQ: AMZN) because it failed the majority of my investing parameters. It is plausible to think that Amazon investors bet on other speculative growth investments that cratered. Unless you are in the right place at the right time—an Amazon employee or vendor, for example—it required stakes in several speculative growth stocks that underperformed to discover the needle in the haystack that accelerated from an online bookseller to marketing products representing all letters of the alphabet.

When reading the ever typical buy and sell on the news mania in the financial media, hold a glass apple paperweight up to the comment, so it appears as though illuminating through a Magic 8-Ball. You may find it makes the comments look much more appropriate.

Value and growth combined are referred to as "growth at a reasonable price" or GARP and reminds us this once popular investing strategy was out of favor in the recent growth-dominant bull market. The "at a reasonable price" part of the GARP equation had left the party; the growth component had remained, supplying the elixir.

A sensible assertion is that thoughtful and disciplined investing involves a commitment to valuation. Investors buy securities believing prices are going up by the end of the day, week, year, or decade. So, why do many fail at the valuation part?

An investor who buys the stock of a non-dividend-paying growth company for the earnings risks disappointment. The opportunity lies in the top-line revenue growth at Seattle, Washington-based Amazon. And at the high-profile, non-dividend-paying Silicon Valley stocks such as content streaming pioneer Netflix (NASDAQ: NFLX), and Alphabet (NASDAQ: GOOG, GOOGL), parent of video hosting service YouTube and search powerhouse Google.

The preferred alternative is when searching for an entry point, look at the effect on valuation from macro- or micro-events without attempting to predict specific future outcomes. Avoid price targets, as the speculation disappoints more often than it delights. Say *No, thank you* to schemes, and stick to low-cost, lesser-risk investments in the stocks of quality, dividend-paying companies purchased at realistic prices. Then hold the shares for as long as the business remains wonderful, including forever. The lesson is the triumphant, do-it-yourself investor conducts research and analysis of companies to own. The trading of stocks becomes a mere support vehicle to the primary objective of ownership.

The best advice conveyed to investors who lack the rare DNA of the successful fast money trader—myself included—is to stop placing bets on speculative equities and start investing in quality businesses.

* * *

CHAPTER SIX SUMMARY

On Owning Companies as Opposed to Trading Stocks

- Contribute to society and yourself or your family by owning the common shares of businesses upholding quality and compliance in an unpredictable world.

- Defensive investors prefer companies already growing, discounting any promises of growth from analysts, bloggers, or management.

- In the short term, as well as in the long term, the crowd is almost always wrong. Outperform the market by becoming an informed investor.

- In buying value now, the thoughtful, disciplined, and patient common stock investor benefits from growth later.

■ Stop placing bets on stocks and start investing in companies. This original concept of trading stocks facilitated willing participants to take affordable partial stakes of publicly traded companies. The approach remains the ideal paradigm.

Seven

Buy Fear And Sell Greed

Buy or add common shares on surprise socioeconomic events and market fears. Sell or reduce on surprise company events and market greed.

The intelligent value investor purchases a slice of a stable company with strong fundamentals when the market is retreating based on fear, then divests or reduces the holding when the market gets greedy and overbuys the stock despite weaker fundamentals or an inflated stock price when microeconomic events erode the financial strength of the company or the demand for its products and services.

Buy on fear and sell on greed, assuming the share price is attractive or above your cost basis. Erratic market corrections such as the COVID-19 coronavirus pandemic notwithstanding, the market prefers to entertain the purchase of attractive fundamentals at high prices and narrow margins of safety. As a result, in the later stages of the post-Great Recession epic bull market, The Model Portfolio had evolved into more of a watch list than a buy list.

This chapter defines the macro and microeconomic impacts of intelligent investing.

Attempts at Market Predictions is a Fool's Game

When the market timer is wrong—the probable outcome—in predicting a surprise market, industry, or company event, substantial assets are lost because the trader is too long or short. On the other side of the trade, the patient investor is prepared to take advantage of the surprise occurrence by allocating planned cash reserves for new or increased positions in the shares of companies with strong fundamentals.

The disciplined investor takes advantage of depressed prices from the indiscriminate macro event. These surprise incidents, any tragedies notwithstanding, trigger a contrarian's opportunity for the thoughtful individual investor. For example, investors who held, added to, or initiated quality positions following the market crash of 1987, during the dot-com bear market of 2000–2002, or the run-up after the Great Recession of 2007–08 profited from subsequent booming portfolios. The market meltdown from the coronavirus pandemic produced similar opportunities for bargain hunters in March of 2020. A few did predict these events, and perhaps each benefited from a stroke of luck. Many investors reacted by selling already depressed securities in the aftermath, and more than a few of these victimized portfolios have yet to recover.

The investor who predicts an impactful market, industry, or company event becomes intoxicated by the lucky call and begins to base an investing philosophy on the sudden perceived ability to foresee future events. Such inebriation of financial intellect induces the proverbial gazing into the crystal ball, encompassing a false state of being. With poetic justice, the luck soon runs out, as does the principal on the investments.

Unless one has the magical instincts of Warren Buffett.

Fear and Greed as Pricing Mechanisms

This chapter supports a value investment theory of becoming greedy from the fear by buying when a surprise macro event affects an entire economy or sector and being fearful of the greed by selling on the surprise micro event limited to a company or industry. Widely credited to Buffett, the metaphor of buying fear and selling greed produced the most famous value investor of our time.

The lesson is another reminder for the independent investor to stop market timing or stock trading and start investing or divesting as macro and microeconomic conditions dictate. Such discipline requires a contrarian's retreat from the crowd. The thoughtful value investor sticks to the tried-and-true approach of researching the fundamentals of the targeted business to determine the potential level of ownership worthiness. And, if warranted, measures the valuation multiples of the underlying stock to decide whether to initiate, add to, maintain, reduce, or sell the holding.

The patient value investor is steadfast in waiting for random macroeconomic events that often lead to fearful retreats from stocks on Wall Street. As prices drop to attractive valuations, sift your watchlist for superb companies with sound fundamentals trading at appealing multiples offering what you perceive as sufficient margins of safety.

As an alternative, add dry powder to your present holdings, as the first and seventh ideas already sitting in your portfolio are perhaps a better value than a new investment opportunity presented by the market. And whenever greed prevails—thereby affecting the valuation or the fundamentals of a single holding—consider reducing or eliminating your ownership in the position at a profit. On the other side of the investment, if the microeconomic event or trader-induced fears render valuations with perceived wide margins of safety, purchase a new stake or add to the position.

In the wake of fear and greed, the value investor reemerges to take advantage of rare opportunities to initiate new positions because quality enterprises seldom trade in the bargain-basement bin except in the aftermath of market downturns. To paraphrase Buffett, as the bull market tide goes out, the junk equity holders are left swimming naked.

If you buy a quality company at a favorable price and the value proposition of the enterprise remains intact, why sell other than to fund new opportunities or finance an upcoming milestone in life with the proceeds?

Again, the value-based investor has the temperament of a contrarian.

Buying is Exhilarating; Selling is Exacerbating

An overlooked challenge for any investor is when to sell a holding. Execute a sell order to deliver profits with a more proactive and less reactive well-thought-out decision process. The occasional *It was a good idea at the time* investment sometimes leads to unloading the persistent underperforming equity to cut further losses.

The fundamentals-driven value investor sells or reduces a slice of the business if it no longer supports the investment thesis.

There was a time when I sold the stocks of companies as much as I bought them. The share prices of many of the sold-out companies are higher today. Selling a stock out of fear of current or future events often works against the best interest of the investor. Just ask Apple (AAPL) shareholders—including yours truly—who went bearish based on Wall Street analyst forecasts following the death of its founder and icon Steve Jobs in 2011.

Hence, it is an obligation as the innkeeper to write follow-up alerts on the common shares held in The Model Portfolio as evolving fundamentals and metrics dictate. It is important to remember that long-term results are the best barometer of equity performance to the dedicated, individual investor. You don't need to chase quarterly performance, as do many of the players on Wall Street and the hordes of followers on Main Street. For this reason, as stated in the investment objectives of *Build Wealth with Common Stocks* and The Model Portfolio and elaborated in Chapter Five, patience is the value investor's best friend.

Sell to Take Profits — Not Quell Emotions

These days, I sell less often, having learned repeated buying and selling underwrite the Wall Street fee machine more than positive returns from my portfolio. I had sold out three stocks represented in The Model Portfolio during the post-Great Recession bull market. Murphy's Law had the price of two up significantly before the COVID-19 coronavirus correction.

When buying enduring quality companies at reasonable prices, there are fewer incentives to sell other than to perhaps finance an essential milestone in life. Take profits on a long-held common stock to finance college tuition, a wedding, a home purchase, a business start-up, or retirement. Your approach to investing in common stocks must be cognitive. Other than the appropriate celebration or brief pity party, there is limited room for feelings and emotions in successful investing.

During the epic 2009 to 2020 bull market, individual securities continued to show attractive fundamentals and enticing dividends; however, prices were steep concerning acceptable valuations and margins of safety. Regardless of how we measure the subjective estimation of intrinsic value, the stock prices appeared stretched. Perhaps the market will keep climbing. Who knows?

Then, the coronavirus pandemic arrived out of left field.

Counter to the heightened impatience in the Wall Street arena, practice patient risk management by waiting for prices of quality stocks to drop to acceptable levels. Avoid predicting specific macro events you have limited control over, and leave the erratic behavior to speculators who own the equities or hold the bonds of companies with suspect business models.

When the surprise event does happen, it is often a buying opportunity for the common shares of quality companies prevailing despite the temporary economic or industry downturn. The disciplined value investor is inclined to wait for the economy's macro- or company micro-events to deflate the stock to a bargain price.

Also, be cautious of the price fluctuations of commodities such as energy, basic food ingredients, and precious metals, to name a few examples. Although enticing to the investor with a Type-A personality, such commodity pricing is often determined from legal manipulation by the producers or traders, thereby transcending the basic economic theory of supply and demand.

The disciplined investor on Main Street, with an occasional exception, avoids direct investment in commodities or the companies in the energy and materials sectors producing and marketing raw materials. Invest in companies as opposed to pricing arbitrage. Be willing to take ownership of businesses that use commodities to manufacture useful products, or else you risk eliminating a broad sampling of quality, publicly traded enterprises.

Insiders Trading and Buybacks

It does amaze how C-suites and boards of directors house some of the worse value investors in the contexts of managing buybacks and stock options. I stopped tracking insider selling some time ago because what motivates each private exercise or sale is unknown. The reasons may include: options are expiring, tuition is due, a new vacation home waits, a director's board term is up, or the seller's wealth manager is recommending portfolio diversification beyond the company stock. The motives to exercise options and sell holdings are endless.

As a real-world example: I had been the fortunate recipient of stock options in a former career, which colleagues and I sold at various times for personal reasons. I noticed an uptick in company-wide sales disclosures when a blanket option grant was vesting or expiring, regardless of the performance or prospects of the business at the time.

Instead, focus on companies with believable value propositions whose stocks are trading at sensible prices despite market forecasters trying to steer you elsewhere. The skepticism of the prognosticators, including followers, creates any temporary mispricing. Why the rampant commitments to this narrow approach?

In twenty years of studying, observing, and practicing equity investing through trial and error, buying the value-priced common shares of quality enterprises is the one path that has been profitable with consistency. The lesson: One cannot sell an overpriced bull to a value-minded butcher.

In the Pursuit of Quality

During the research of this book, the Wall Street consensus appeared as an overheated bull market where speculation ruled, and valuations went ignored. Shorts were perhaps the exception, although engaged in speculative activity, nonetheless. As a result of the climate, portfolios were performing more as watch lists than buy lists. Hence, continue to seek excellent, publicly traded companies with strong fundamentals inspiring you to take part as a proud owner. Be an advocate of the companies harboring quality products or services and consistent profitability.

The lesson is to practice patience and discipline in advance of the unpredictable surprise macroeconomic event or the market's fearful retreat from stocks. Each juncture presents an ideal opportunity to add targeted dividend-paying common shares of select enterprises to your portfolio.

Call me an idealist, but I prefer contributing to society and my family by taking an ownership slice of a company providing quality and value to a world starving for each. Great businesses always find ways to endure by surviving internal micro issues or external macroeconomic and geopolitical events. Since the pursuit of quality plus value works well in many areas of our lives, it is essential to include investing in the realm.

Never celebrate macro and microeconomic events and the inevitable harm each does to fellow workers or investors who become the unfortunate victims of an affected economy, sector, stock, natural disaster, or health crisis. Instead, revisit your portfolio and watch list and commence new research to look for individual companies where strong fundamentals, sensible valuations, and comfortable margins of safety merge in a rare perfect storm of opportunity. As an everyday investor on Main Street, it is your inherent responsibility to be greedy when the market is fearful. And when the market or management gets greedy in an invested company or industry, reverse course and reduce or sell off as key metrics dictate.

Pursue alpha with large doses of rationale, saving any emotion to celebrate successes or assess failures after the trade — never before. The lesson for the independent investor is to stop market timing or stock trading and start investing or divesting as macro and microeconomic conditions dictate. Such a contrarian's retreat from the crowd requires the accumulation of the rarest of commodities: thought, common sense, patience, and discipline.

CHAPTER SEVEN SUMMARY

On Fear and Greed

- The value-based investor takes advantage of pricing mechanisms produced from fear and greed.

- Purchase the common shares of excellent companies with strong fundamentals when macroeconomic events or market fear drive down the ticker prices. Sell or reduce the holdings when microeconomic events or market greed weaken the fundamentals or the demand for the products and services.

- The thoughtful common stock investor never attempts to predict a market, industry, or company event and instead prepares to take advantage of any surprises after the fact.

- Great businesses find ways to endure by surviving external macroeconomic and geopolitical events or internal micro issues.

- Whether shaped by geopolitical, market, industry, or company events, investment and divestment opportunities are present through every market cycle.

Eight

Hedge As An Alternative To Indexing

What is the best alternative to do-it-yourself, active investing? The financial media suggests investing in passive indexes to guarantee your portfolio at least keeps pace with the market.

What is the worst choice? Joining the crowd and trading the short-sighted gimmicks churned out by the Wall Street fee machine is inferior to passive indexing and buy-and-hold common stock investing.

It is typical for the proponents of passive investing to omit a reminder that indexes contain every company in the market, sector, or industry, translating to owning a lot of poor-quality enterprises in addition to the few good ones. Thus, the superior investor limits the holding of an index exchange-traded fund (ETF) to hedging the common stocks in a portfolio with designs to outperform the market benchmark over time.

The material in this chapter explores the general concept of portfolio hedging—albeit on the long side—and why it is essential to any active, long-term investment strategy.

Using Passive Index ETFs to Hedge a Portfolio

Index ETFs provide the retail investor passively managed funds of publicly traded equities or fixed-income securities. Although safer, in theory, than individual stocks, passive index ETFs carry the shared risks of any equity investing, including the loss of invested capital because of fund company failures, irrational market sentiment, negative financial news, or surprise events.

Passive indexing assures average returns to the market, for better or worse. Index ETFs tend to be less vulnerable to volatility and market liquidity than individual stocks. Thus, the best investing purpose for index ETFs is as a portfolio hedge against a basket of related or conflicting individual stocks as far as market, industry, or capitalization.

When used for hedging, passive index ETFs offer the longer-view retail investor the opportunity for strategic diversification toward a safer portfolio. Diversification presents as a two-edged sword, leaving the over-diversified common stock portfolio best served by passive indexing to lessen risk and lower costs. In contrast, concentrated portfolios of the common stocks of select quality companies—hedged by distribution-paying ETF compounders each purchased at reasonable prices—provide the best opportunity for success for the long-term retail investor. Suggesting that an active individual investor go 100 percent index funds is akin to recommending that an avid angler buy every fish at the market.

Funds of companies cannot assure that each enterprise represented carries the preceding qualitative parameters. Buying individual common stocks gives the retail investor more control over the quality of the holdings in the portfolio. Nevertheless, even a well-planned and executed long-term value-based portfolio needs to hedge against the inevitable ups and downs of the market. The daily news cycle and quarterly earnings reports drive the speculators to buy, sell, and short recklessly. Be on guard against the unpredictable, although inevitable, external threats to your holdings.

Whether used for active or passive investing, exchange-traded funds, or ETFs, are derivatives notorious for inherent risk from massive investor participation. Warren Buffett has said that makes them candidates for "financial weapons of mass destruction"[1] in a down market. Therefore, the defensive hedge positioning of choice is the secondary use of indexed exchange-traded funds.

Look to Vanguard Group for ETF Hedges

Because beating the market with consistency is the Achilles' heel of the active investor—inclusive of the Wall Street money manager elite—hedge your portfolio on the long side using indexed ETFs tracking the relevant benchmarks. Of note, index ETFs do have lower fees on average than mutual funds. By hedging with an ETF, the thoughtful investor enhances the risk/reward proposition.

On occasion, I have deployed three ETF hedges in our family portfolio: Vanguard Short-Term Inflation-Protected Securities ETF (NYSE: VTIP), Vanguard FTSE All-World ex-US ETF (NYSE: VEU), and Vanguard S&P 500 ETF (NYSE: VOO).

Hedging with the short-duration bonds of US Treasury inflation-protected securities, such as Vanguard's VTIP, with the stocks of non-US companies, such as Vanguard's VEU, and with the S&P 500 as represented in Vanguard's VOO, allows the retail investor to keep pace with the voting machine turbulence of the market in the short-run. Then, focus with confidence on the capital gains and dividend payouts of the weighing machine over time. Each is an excellent choice to hedge against periods when those distinct markets outperform your basket of select common stocks.

I chose Vanguard for ETF hedges because, as a mutual-owned enterprise, it is immune to answering to independent stockholders or outside owners. The objective of Vanguard is to manage each fund at cost, allowing investors to keep more of the returns. The benefits of Vanguard align with the three primary investment objectives of *Build Wealth with Common Stocks*.

- Limited capital: Vanguard's publicly traded ETFs have no criteria for investment minimums beyond the price of one share.

- Lower costs: At the time of writing this chapter, VTIP carried an annual expense ratio of just 0.05 percent; VEU was a respectable 0.08 percent; VOO was the lowest at 0.03 percent. By using a commission-free online discount broker, you pay pennies for the occasional ETF trade.

- Less risk: VTIP, as a short-duration government bond fund, carried a low-risk rating; the international exposure of VEU was earning an average risk rating; VOO as a domestic stock market benchmark also had an average risk rating.

The mutual ownership approach to the investment products of Vanguard satisfies the crux of the mantra of this book in building and maintaining wealth with limited capital, lower costs, and less risk. The three ETF hedges were each paying distributions—the cumulative quarterly dividends or bond yields, plus occasional capital gains from the holdings in the ETF—and offered low portfolio turnover.

Invest in the common shares of quality companies hedged with passive index ETFs through low-cost, online discount brokers and mutual investment companies such as Vanguard.

Protect Your Portfolio Against Inflationary Cycles

Although deflated interest rates were a boon for equities in the 2009 to 2020 bull market, the ongoing threat to the stock market is inflation — the annualized spike in the price of goods, services, and interest rates. The contrarian thinks of hyperinflation as the third worse menace to the market after high fees from the financial services industry and illogical investor sentiment from the crowd.

Inflation-protected securities, such as VTIP, offer protection against hyperinflation as a potential stock market killer, producing a bounty for the value investor. The objective of short-duration bonds is to provide lower real interest rate risk over several market cycles until acute inflationary pressure rears its head. Nonetheless, we have limited control over trader and investor behavior beyond taking an opposing stance to the irrational investing or divesting by the herd. On the contrary, it is possible to protect our portfolios from unexpected inflation spikes.

Because of historic low-interest rates and deflation, TIPs—Treasury inflation-protected securities—had been a non-story in the great bull market. Forever contrarian, the value investor knows the best time to buy inflation hedges, regardless of the vehicle of choice, is when inflation is off Wall Street's radar. Traditional inflation hedges had become less expensive as the fast money gobbled up high-yield dividend and non-dividend growth stocks, as well as cryptocurrency.

This chapter is perhaps a simple exercise in value investing because when inflation strikes again, investors will load up on inflation-protected products en masse, whether short-duration bonds, precious metals, or real estate, at much higher entry prices.

What about diversifying a retail portfolio with fixed income, such as bonds or bond funds?

Throughout the second decade of this century, the mainstream financial media was reporting that intermediate and long-duration fixed-income debt instruments—government or corporate-issued bonds, bills, or notes—were a bubble waiting to burst. The extended bull market in bonds dated back to the 1980s, ground zero for borrowing our way to prosperity in America. This self-defeating economic insanity continued forty years later.

Whether in business or at home, consider the accumulation of debt your most significant threat. Strategic debt is beneficial for building foundations in our professional or personal lives, whereas indebtedness to finance an immediate sense of prosperity is often a death knell.

As such, in The Model Portfolio, I favor equity ownership to lending by investing in stocks as opposed to bonds. I also accept that using short-duration Treasury bills as a hedge plays a crucial role in helping to protect the portfolio against the perils of hyperinflation when it occurs.

Double-Down the Hedge

The Model Portfolio represents a concentrated mix of common stocks purchased or available on the two major US exchanges: the Nasdaq Stock Market (NASDAQ) and the New York Stock Exchange (NYSE). Covering the broader market, I benchmark the portfolio against the S&P 500, the citadel of publicly traded American enterprises.

When deployed, the passive Vanguard S&P 500 ETF (VOO) represents the benchmark hedge of The Model Portfolio. At unpredictable times when the portfolio underperforms the S&P 500, VOO picks up the slack.

Although representing companies serving the globe, The Model Portfolio holdings, for the most part, are domiciled in the United States. Therefore, I prefer hedging the basket with the FTSE All-World ex-US Index. The index captures the performance of major exchange-traded companies domiciled outside of the US, and as an independent investor, I never regret taking a globalist view.

My objective is to own an international index as protection against volatility in domestic stocks as opposed to an investment in and of itself. The preferred ETF allocation for foreign hedging is Vanguard's VEU.

VOO and VEU are market-cap-weighted, the prevailing, if controversial, weighing mechanism. Market cap or capitalization-weighted indexes assign component value by the total market value of the outstanding shares against the cumulative market cap of the index. Thus, the highest market cap stock in the index has the maximum influence on the net asset value of the security.

There are other weighting mechanisms, such as price-weighted, equal-weighted, and fundamental-weighted. The Dow Jones Industrial Average uses price weighting, where the higher-priced components receive the maximum weight. Equal-weight treats each constituent the same regardless of price or market cap. Fundamental weight employs metrics such as sales, book value, dividends, cash flow, and earnings. Active ETF investors seeking faster growth often turn to alternative weighting methods in an attempt to hedge any increase in risk.

In a market-weighted index, mega-cap companies dominate a significant portion of the index. For example, in the S&P 500, it is normal for the top ten components to represent over 20 percent of the basket. On the contrary, in the FTSE All-World ex-US, such as VEU, the ten largest holdings represented fewer than 10 percent of net assets.

Instead of owning as an outright investment, the objective of the foreign index is protection against the volatility of the concentrated portfolio of domestic stocks. Again, if you want to be an above-average investor, limit any exposure to the S&P 500 or FTSE All-World ex-US indices to hedging. Index hedges are investments by proxy complete with inherent risks, including loss of principal. On the other side of the risk/reward equation, you take profits from the distributions of the index ETFs as well. Nevertheless, each is foremost a hedge on the long side.

The disciplined value investor is less concerned with NAV—net asset value—or premium discounts on ETFs exploited by arbitrage traders seeking a short-term mispricing edge than a more suitable long-term inflation protection or market hedge.

Assets under management in index ETFs have ballooned in recent years. The phenomenon concerns market pundits who believe sizable derivative-driven ETFs such as passive index funds—and perhaps more the speculative leveraged ETFs—will implode or outright trigger a catastrophic financial event in a market correction. Index ETFs are safer as opposed to safe.

Personal Values Drive Politics — Dollar Values Drive Portfolios

Along with owning US companies, whether operating as a domestic or as a multinational, sound portfolio strategy includes hedging with foreign-based companies. The stock holdings of international companies, such as represented by the Vanguard VEU ETF, are a wise global hedge against US-domiciled publicly traded companies.

The recent populist sentiment toward protectionism and national-ism provides a feel-good platform to generate votes on Election Day with heated debate in the comments of online news feeds and social me-dia. Nationalism and protectionism in the near term aside, globalization and its multinational product and service demand indeed prevail in the long run.

My father shared this thought with me just months before he passed away: "You cannot stop progress, although many forever attempt to bring us back to the 'way things used to be.' From a historical perspec-tive, if regressive thinking was successful in halting progress, we'd still be living in caves."

Whether or not one empathizes with my father's transformative ex-perience of the world he was about to depart, carrying a conviction of nationalist sentiment to our portfolios sabotages investment opportu-nities in the global markets. Or, at the least, hedging strategies to pro-tect against our inherent bias toward the stocks of US-based companies. Warren Buffet has promoted a strong bull market case for S&P 500 components over the long term, and I advocate international exposure at least as a protection against potential US bear markets in the near term.

Politics sometimes validates our values, including emotional attach-ments to the domestic bliss of American exceptionalism. Our portfolios are best served by rational thinking and an acceptance of globalization as a sound diversification strategy.

Indexing is for Passive Investors

From an apparent noble concern for the Main Street investor and de-spite active participation in the markets, Wall Street gurus often ad-vocate passive investing—via mutual or exchange-traded funds—as the best overall strategy for retail investors.

Indexing is appropriate for passive investors with less interest in self-directed investing or limited trust in the alternative of a fee-and-bonus-focused money manager. For the retail-level investor, passive indexing guarantees your portfolio performance averages to the market, at best. In the spirit of *Build Wealth with Common Stocks*, using index ETFs to hedge an active portfolio strategy, as opposed to an outright investment, is perhaps the best route in the quest for total return from capital gains and dividends.

Laser your focus on major exchange-traded, common stocks. Avoid the speculative risk associated with illiquid micro caps, defined as lower than $1 billion in market capitalization. In the FOMO-influenced post-Great Recession bull market, micro caps represented over 70 percent of publicly traded companies on the exchanges, both major and over-the-counter (OTC). OTC is defined as traded via a broker/dealer network instead of a centralized exchange.

Investing in OTC issues—predominated by foreign-based enterprises—is speculative at best. Passing on the unnecessary risk forces the investor to miss out on an international staple or two; however, the OTC listing represents the underlying security more than the actual business operation. Perhaps a savvy individual investor is best served by opening a brokerage account that allows the purchase of primary common stock on the major exchange of the country where the company is domiciled. Such an approach adds the challenge of currency exchange rates.

Owning US exchange-traded common shares representing companies paying dividends far outweighs the risks of perceived fast money opportunities from the micro caps and OTCs. Consider keeping your major exchange-traded, non-dividend-paying growth stock allocation to a minimum. Quality dividend stocks compensate you now with regular payouts and reward you later with compounding capital gains. Nonetheless, discipline is an absolute must in choosing to dismiss trend following and momentum stocks, as no one enjoys watching the prices of familiar yet unowned tickers go up with abandon, as happened in the epic bull market. The solace lies in the stomach-turning volatility of the upticks and downslides.

Many unknowing investors lose principal when these speculative stocks, unsupported by sound fundamentals or attractive valuations, take sudden steep price drops. Not unlike the enthusiastic casino gambler, retail investors who chase fast money brag when winning. Yet, unlike the veiled poor gaming results, the vulnerable securities tickers dance across televisions, desktops, and mobile screens.

Increase the chances of tooting your horn more often by owning slices of quality companies paying sensible dividends that keep you compensated in the short-term as you wait for capital appreciation of the underlying stock over the long term. Hedge those capital gains and dividends with quality passive index ETFs, such as VTIP, VEU, and VOO from Vanguard when the prices are right.

Buy the Best Stocks in the Sector

Don't buy the sector; buy the best stocks in the sector. Allocate your investment cash to the mispriced stocks of quality companies instead of an equity index or intermediate or long-duration bond fund other than for hedging.

Use equity ETFs as hedges against single company holdings for the expected ups and downs of a market cycle. Avoid using equity index ETFs to hedge against a stock market crash or a prolonged downturn, as each will race to the bottom along with the market. Others promote commodities, precious metals, cryptocurrency, bonds, and more complicated instruments designed to hedge inflation. FDIC-insured cash remains an ideal hedge against market capitulation as cash is the safest alternative other than avoiding equities in general, thus guaranteeing we become below-average, or worse, investors. Therefore, focus on bottom-up equity analysis, finding value in mispriced single ticker stocks that you deem the best in the sector.

To Index or Not to Index

Warren Buffett's blanket suggestion of passive indexing for Main Street, notwithstanding, a perpetual head-scratcher is the overall recurrent criticism of Buffett in the financial media. The censure is analogous to finding fault in Albert Einstein, Mark Twain, Martin Luther King Jr., Mother Theresa, or Nelson Mandela. Yes, as in any human, the flaws are there; however, the condemnation appears more as unsubstantiated fear, hate, anger, or envy than a sincere attempt at intellectual critique.

The suggestion for universal indexing on Main Street emanates from others than just Buffett; it often comes from professional investors who share exploits in the financial media. Each buys or shorts stocks, funds, fixed income, options, futures, and derivatives and writes about such ventures following a winning trade, and then tells the reader to buy an index. It is as if the professional has a special Wall Street VIP card of some kind.

And this is where Buffett and his wisdom come back to center court. If these pundits, to whom he offers the more eloquent constructive criticism, beat the market with consistency, the perceived contempt of the investing elite appears as sincere good advice. Since most underperform, it confirms their feeble attempt at covert prose instead of overt results.

To be fair, if a retail investor finds comfort in the safety of average returns, limiting portfolio holdings to the ever-prevalent passive index funds remains a wise choice. Instead of attempting to time the market, consider hedging your portfolio against the likelihood of an irrational herd mentality or less predictable events such as hyperinflation and economic downturns. These words of wisdom from Howard Marks speak volumes: "Following the beliefs of the herd will give you average performance in the long run and can get you killed at the extremes."[2]

First, buy the high-quality, reasonably-priced stocks in your sectors of choice; second, hedge the portfolio with passive index ETFs.

* * *

CHAPTER EIGHT SUMMARY

On Hedging versus Passive Indexing with ETFs

- Passive index investing assures average returns to the market, whereas hedging a portfolio of common stocks with low-cost exchange-traded funds provides increased diversification and safety.

- If hedging your portfolio, the index ETFs from Vanguard Group are wise choices because, as a mutual-owned enterprise, it is immune to independent stockholders or outside owners.

- FDIC-insured cash is the safest hedge against market capitulation.

- Investing in the common shares of quality international ex-US companies is noble indeed, as despite nationalism and protectionism dominating the news cycle, globalization, driven by multinational product and service demand, prevails in the long run.

- The thoughtful investor buys slices of the best companies in the sector, reserving the entire universe for hedging.

Nine

Create Wealth With Total Return

C hasing dividend yields and non-dividend growth are recipes for junk. Build wealth with total-return investing—capital gains plus income—thus, in retirement, you are pursuing bucket list items instead of higher dividend payouts.

I rebalance our family portfolio perhaps once a year—by adjusting the holdings to maintain asset allocation—driving it as a total-return vehicle as opposed to one of income-only. Remember, dividends keep you compensated in the short term as you wait for capital appreciation of the stock over time.

This chapter explains why and how total return best serves the thoughtful, disciplined, and patient investor.

Practice Total-Return Investing

Quality dividend value investing, or total return, focuses on dividend yields below 5 percent, a range where you find superior companies paying far lower than 100 percent of earnings in dividends, also referred to as the payout ratio, addressed later in this chapter. Many companies behind 6 to 10 percent and higher-yielding shares must grow dividend rates, or the stocks need to fall in price, or a combination thereof for the dividend yields to remain high or increase. Those are recipes for disaster.

It is rare for popular trends to become remedies for struggling investors. Time and again, each investment fad is harmful to portfolios. As discussed in Part II, Chapter Twelve, the thoughtful investor favors companies where the average of trailing dividend yields plus the yields on earnings and free cash flow exceed the prevailing Ten-Year Treasury rate. Nevertheless, we cannot predict the future with accuracy and never attempt to do so at the expense of your portfolio and the family it supports.

Although safer than high-yield dividend or non-dividend growth investing, dividend-paying value investing carries the shared risks of investing in the stock market. All dividend stocks face unexpected rate reductions or suspensions by the board of directors of the company. The dividend-paying common shares of quality companies tend to be less vulnerable to ticker price volatility and market liquidity than high-yield dividend or non-dividend growth stocks.

All the Rage for the Wrong Reasons

High-yield dividend stocks were top-of-mind for investors starving for higher payouts in the low-interest-rate environment of the post-Great Recession bull market. Many top subscription offerings and financial media pieces focused on the high-yield paradigm. History tells us the crowd is almost always wrong when it comes to fads and favorites. High-yield dividend stocks—defined as 6 percent and higher yields on common shares—are no exception, and that is why I maintain a perpetual bearish view.

Along with high returns, loom risky headwinds and questionable underlying fundamentals. Just ask the victims of the high-yield junk bond bubble in the 1980s. Perhaps the recent bull market and its high-yield equity opportunities are different; the perma bulls rejoice.

The junk bond craze returned to the recent bull market in the form of high-yield dividend stocks. And history reminds us how that bubble burst during the stock market crash of 1987. This time, instead of leveraging mergers and acquisitions at the corporate level when available capital was insufficient, high-yield equities influenced daring risk/reward plays as retail investors and advisors sought outsized returns to leverage retirement account balances.

Defining high-yield equity is debatable and broad. Therefore, this chapter distinguishes high-yield dividend stocks as publicly traded equities distributing at least three times the Ten-Year Treasury rate that stood at a 1.92 percent yield as of December 31, 2019. Hence, we arrive at 6 percent or higher as our arguable definition of high-yield equity. In the context of the COVID-19 pandemic, consider the sub-1 percent rates of 2020 an anomaly.

An inevitable cyclical downturn in the overall stock market preempts the principal capital invested by millions of retail investors concentrated in risky, high-yield dividend equities such as business development companies (BDCs), master limited partnerships (MLPs), and real estate investment trusts (REITs). The thoughtful investor never buys stocks based on market euphoria or the dividend yield alone.

His Neighbor Yelled, "Buy the Yield"

For some background: High-yield dividend investing appeared on my radar earlier in the post-Great Recession bull market from a retired family member. Acting on a tip from a neighbor—mistake number one—he moved a substantial amount of capital from a well-known, blue-chip equity REIT to the unpriced, non-marketable security of a high-yielding hotel REIT.

The REIT staple sold out to create the capital ended up a seven-bagger stock with an approximate range of 4 to 5 percent in average annual dividends in the subsequent years. As promised, the unpriced hotel REIT paid much higher dividends, and the security in due course went public at about the original cost per share. On the precipice of the COVID-19 coronavirus correction, the price of the now publicly traded hotel REIT was down 15 percent since the IPO, although it continued to pay healthy dividends. An inadequate result in the scheme of things, as it equated to a no bagger, in stark contrast to the seven times return of the blue-chip REIT sold to create capital for the high-yield, unpriced security.

The misfortune of the family member is an example of the risks involved with unpriced securities. Whether priced or unpriced, the persuasion of retirees to sell below 5 percent stable yielders for the 6 to 10 percent plus yields of risky equities was widespread. Again, caveat emptor prevails.

The enticement of high yields on a stock seems to overshadow the necessary due diligence required to determine if the representative company is stable enough to justify the yield with capital allocations and shareholder returns from a well-managed operation. Do we prefer to own a quality 4 percent yielder with compounding average capital gains of 6 percent a year, or a high-risk stock yielding 10 percent, although averaging a minus 5 percent annualized capital loss?

In the former, the value investor is averaging a plus 10 percent average annual total gain. In contrast, the high-yield fan is settling for a meager plus 5 percent average annual total return.

Perhaps some retirees have had the exact opposite experience by investing in high yielders producing double-digit total returns each year during the recent bull market. Similar to a raucous party, this bubble burst as well when the coronavirus pandemic arrived uninvited. High-dividend investors who think it possible to time the perfect exit are sailing on the proverbial ship of fools.

Chasing Yield: A Recipe for Junk

Many top financial advisors, bloggers, and investors focus research and investing energies in high-yield dividend investing, such as REITs, BDCs, and other closed-end funds (CEFs), as well as energy transfer partnerships and preferred stocks.

For those wondering why the book is exclusive to common shares, preferred stock is an equity instrument presenting as a glorified bond with emphasis on the dividend. Despite holding no voting rights, preferred shareholders are paid a piece of the earnings before the common shareholders. If you are committed to owning minuscule slices of quality companies, there is less worry about getting in line for payment. Thus, take the secondary dividend and the first voting rights—and, more important, the capital gains— of the common shares of high-quality, enduring companies.

Some well-crafted story headlines and marketing pitches cast a positive spin on the paradox of a safe, high yielder. Such absurdity is akin to fishing for sushi-grade salmon in a crystal clear river known as toxic from a colorless pollutant.

As expected, these pundits remind me of what I missed, disregarded, and tripped over in the amateur analysis, challenging some of my assumptions and conclusions. Although the professional debate is encouraged and welcome, my thesis remains that investors are chasing the dividend more than enterprise quality with high-yield stocks. Nonetheless, if a conscientious trading strategy is putting income ahead of capital gains, so be it with cautionary best wishes.

Remember, dividend rates adjust on a monthly, quarterly, or annual basis from board-directed payouts; and the corresponding yields go up and down each market day as a prisoner of the stock price. The concept of dividend payouts involves a simple paradigm in the fundamental economics of the price/yield relationship, whether bonds or equities. When the price goes up, the yield goes down, and vice versa.

The Alternative High-Yield Dividend Model

Measure a stock holding's yield on cost as opposed to chasing current dividend payouts. The return on cost represents the yield of the current dividend rate relative to the cost basis of the common shares. For example, as of the June 30, 2020, quarterly update, the yield on cost of each of the five original holdings of The Model Portfolio was far superior to the current forward yield.

Ticker	Closing Price	Dividend Rate	Cost Basis	Forward Yield	Yield-to-Cost
DIS	$111.51	$1.76	$20.88	1.58%	8.43%
MMM	$155.99	$5.88	$63.15	3.77%	9.31%
UNP	$169.07	$3.88	$29.26	2.29%	13.26%
KO	$44.68	$1.64	$20.71	3.67%	7.92%
MSFT	$203.51	$2.04	$20.87	1.00%	9.77%

Yield on Cost of The Model Portfolio's Original Five Holdings
Source: The Model Portfolio at davidjwaldron.com. Period ending June 30, 2020.

Table Key

- Ticker — Walt Disney (DIS), 3M (MMM), Union Pacific (UNP), Coca-Cola (KO), and Microsoft (MSFT).
- Closing Price — Closing share price on June 30, 2020.
- Dividend Rate — Trailing one-year dividend payout.
- Cost Basis — Original cost of each common share of stock adjusted for splits and dividends.
- Forward Yield — Dividend rate divided by closing share price.
- Yield on Cost — Dividend rate divided by cost basis per share.

Payout Ratio

The payout ratio is the proportion of earnings paid out as dividends to shareholders, expressed as a percentage. A lower payout ratio is preferable to a higher one; a rate higher than 100 percent indicates the company is paying out more in dividends than it earns in net income. Many of the inflated payout players are REITs and BDCs, required by financial laws and regulations to distribute up to 90 percent of taxable income to shareholders. I screened high-yield dividend stocks, and more than 50 percent of the companies listed had payout ratios higher than 100 percent. Where is the cash flow to support this generosity?

The concern is whether the excess payout is coming from somewhere on the balance sheet or cash flow statement detrimental to the financial stability of the operation. Instead of chasing risky, high-yield dividends, calculate the yield on cost on your current holdings with low payout ratios. The five holdings of The Model Portfolio showcased in the preceding yield on cost table had payout ratios of between 32 and 77 percent.

Seek companies paying sustainable and predictable dividends to shareholders, as those payments will keep you compensated in the short-term as you wait patiently for the capital appreciation of the stock price over the long term. Own a quality company with a sensible payout ratio, and the dividend yield will take care of itself.

Despite the popularity of high yield, become an advocate for the ownership of quality companies represented by dividend-paying common stocks listed on US major exchanges and available at value prices. In retirement, the dividend becomes income in itself. And when measured by the yield on cost, your low payout ratio dividend may be earning a high yield worthy of ownership.

Outperform the Market or Join It

The do-it-yourself, active approach to building wealth with commons stocks is about outperforming across each market cycle, whether bull, bear, or range-bound.

Among my favorite individual investors included my wife's, Aunt Beverly. She bought and held stocks leaving the share certificates in a bank vault and never selling. Her broker made a pittance off Beverly's lifelong pursuit, and a few of her holdings had gone to zero. Nevertheless, by the end of her life, the portfolio delivered a powerful lesson in the potential rewards of buying and holding the common shares of wonderful companies and enjoying the compounding total return of capital and dividends.

A humble reminder that it is possible to outperform the S&P 500 over an extended timeline. If a retiree, the priority is perhaps to hold stable, blue-chip businesses providing safe cash flows from dividends that are exceeding the prevailing inflation rate. Remember, instead of serving the market—as many investors do—allow the market to serve you.

Model the portfolios of successful retail investors, such as Aunt Beverly, who reminds us the total return paradigm produces some of the most exceptional performances in common stock investing. As low-fee generators, those portfolios are hard to find on Wall Street. Such practices force us to build portfolios on our own with limited capital, although at lower costs and less risk.

CHAPTER NINE SUMMARY

On Creating Wealth from Total-Return Value Investing

- High-yield dividend stocks and dividend growth investing were all the rage in the post-Great Recession bull market for all the wrong reasons.

- The thoughtful, disciplined, and patient investor is steadfast to dividend value investing or total return from capital gains and dividend income.

- Mistake number one for many investors is buying into an investment based on a tip from a broker, financial writer, or worse, a neighbor. Do your research.

- A profitable alternative to high-yield investing is calculating the yield on cost of quality companies with low payout ratios already residing in your portfolio.

- Instead of chasing yield, buy quality at a reasonable price, and, as Aunt Beverly, hold for as long as you can, perhaps forever. Any dividend payouts are a bonus.

Ten

Embrace An Enduring Market Truth

Value matters in every area of our financial lives, including the stock market. The investment truth endures through each market cycle for decades to come, and perhaps forever. This chapter further explores the virtues of value investing.

Price Is What You Pay — Value Is What You Get

Value investing is an investment paradigm based on the ideas taught by Benjamin Graham and David Dodd at Columbia Business School beginning in 1928 and later published in the 1934 textbook *Security Analysis*.[1] Covered in Part II, Chapter Fourteen, although value investing has taken many forms since its inception, as a rule, it involves buying securities that appear underpriced from fundamental analysis.

> *Ben Graham taught me that "Price is what you pay; value is what you get." Whether we're talking about socks or stocks, I like buying quality merchandise when it is marked down.*[2]
> —WARREN BUFFETT

Today, value investors commit to Graham and Buffett's time-tested wisdom of *price is what you pay; value is what you get*. Despite any compelling fundamental research on the targeted company and its industry, let price drive your final decision to buy shares or pass for now. Finding quality operators in any market is challenging. Uncovering such companies at bargain prices in a bull market is equivalent to finding the proverbial needle in a haystack. Price is what you pay for ownership slices of these high-quality businesses. Value is what you gain over time.

Price and value are paramount to matching or exceeding the stock market's historical average annualized returns from those occasional market pops of big gain days or quarters that underwrite positive long-term gains. Yes, there are intermittent bad days or weeks as well; however, the long-term overall average annualized gains suggest the good days outnumber the bad ones.

Favorite Words of Value Investing Wisdom

A quote from a contributor to the financial website *Seeking Alpha*, who writes under the pseudonym Belgian and Bullish, puts the subject matter of this chapter—and the book—in perspective:

> **"** *For me, time in the market offers more opportunity than try-* **"**
> *ing to time the market.* [3]
> —LEANDER POTTERS, A.K.A. BELGIAN AND BULLISH

Timing the market by chasing trends and fads is for the fast money trader. Time *in* the market, enjoying the magic of compounding total return protected by a wide margin of safety, is for the patient and disciplined investor.

Over 80 percent of the total shares of common stock owned by Americans belong to institutional investors, inclusive of the wealthiest 10 percent of households. Ever the optimist, that leaves almost 20 percent of common stock equity for the rest of us to own and profit from the magic of compounding. Learn to invest in slices of companies as opposed to trading stocks or chasing fast money fads.

Before the coronavirus pandemic, Bitcoin was taxiing to be the next fall from grace. Before that were subprime mortgaged back securities, zero-revenue dot-com IPOs, junk bonds, and land deals in the western United States. I am perhaps missing a few other fast money schemes that fell in between yesterday's barren land, the post-Great Recession bull market's Cryptonite, and the unfortunate pandemic of 2020.

From purely an investment standpoint, there are just a few market timers in each event who got in with a lucky twist of fate or the rare intuitive sense of market conditions, profited, and got out. Those are the ones who dominate the financial news feeds and sponsored content, giving a false appearance of the bullishness or bearishness in the market fad among the masses of well-intentioned investors.

The sobering truth reminds us the money-making headliners represent a tiny percentage of the active participants. Too many players in the fad lose money and, echoing the typical casino gambler, share only the rare winning bets. Just another reminder that market fads make money for a lucky few at the zero-sum expense of the silent investor majority that loses out from the desperate hope to make a lifetime of capital gains in a single market cycle.

The list of household names who made fortunes beating the market by owning investments with utility over extended periods is lengthy. Yet, I am unable to name a celebrity investor, off the top of my head, who adds wealth year in and out on fast money, market-timing fads.

Price is what you pay; value is what you get.

A Superior Investing Paradigm

To this point, the book has accentuated an investment philosophy that avoids estimating or following specific price targets or ranges. Instead, shift your focus and courage to embracing the attractive valuation metrics of wonderful businesses and buy or add whether the shares are trading at $25 or $100.

In the short-term, speculators are buying, selling, or shorting a stock in reaction to current events, expressing confidence or timidity by casting a vote reversed in a moment of breaking news, technical chart swings, or an earnings surprise. In contrast, the investor who takes the long-view will buy, hold, and sometimes sell the shares of a company based on a fundamental analysis of its established history, the estimation of valuation metrics, and the perceived longer-term prospects.

In the spirit of Benjamin Graham, weigh the long-term prospects of the business as opposed to casting a popular vote based on a short-term bias within the market. A stock's endorsement by the contrarian centers on years of actual returns on invested capital and owners' earnings. Your dilemma is contending with the voters contemplating the stock after the quarterly earnings release.

Despite the noise, choose to remain patient as you monitor the prospects of the enterprise while collecting dividends as the short-term reward for your perseverance of awaiting capital appreciation in the longer term.

Expectations derived from a perceived margin of safety are speculative as well. Nonetheless, owning a slice of the well-run casino business for the prospect of profits and asset appreciation over several years is a better bet than gambling on the casino floor tonight in hopes of a quick gain. Capturing value benefits our strategic analysis as partial owners of an enterprise more than the tactical, although fleeting, whim of a stock trade.

Be willing to ride the voting machine bumps and controversies along the way as you await the ultimate results of the weighing machine. As in politics and business, rational thought prevails over irrational emotion for the patient, disciplined, and value-based investor.

Similar to other durable purchases in life, publicly traded stocks are voted in the short-term and weighed in the long-term. In each case, the price is what you pay now; the value is what you acquire over time.

The investment truth endures through every market cycle.

Value Investing is Forever

As widely reported, many in the financial services industry and media consider value investing as dead in the water. I believe value investing is alive and well and lives forever, but what the heck do I know?

Well, I do know that many of the premier investors in modern history are value-oriented. William Browne, Warren Buffett, Mario Gabelli, Benjamin Graham, Joel Greenblatt, Seth Klarman, Peter Lynch, Howard Marks, Bill Miller, Charlie Munger, Michael Price, John W. Rogers Jr., Charles Royce, Walter Schloss, Sir John Templeton, Geraldine Weiss, and Martin Whitman are legends.

These value investor household names remind us the practice of owning the common shares of quality companies with wide margins of safety at the time of purchase is as enduring as rock and roll, electricity, and that Earth is indeed round.

Anything with promise, value investing included—and despite ever-evolving and persevering—has its lapses in popularity or methods of delivery. Nevertheless, there is no equal to value investing for the individual striving to build and maintain an enduring portfolio financing the indispensable milestones in the lives of loved ones.

Although it is essential to underscore that I remain a die-hard value investor, the investment paradigm was out of favor on Wall Street during the momentum growth bull market, making it more challenging to attract readers if the word *value* appeared in the title. In hindsight, I could, would, and should have bought Amazon (AMZN) shares at about $600 when its paid subscription service, Prime, began to take off in 2016. Or Netflix (NFLX) in 2013 for $50 when the company started streaming original content. And Alphabet (GOOG, GOOGL) in 2004 when its IPO was available to retail investors for about $85 a share. Of recent, it has become vogue for long-time celebrity-named value investors to bite the bullet and buy the more speculative, non-dividend-paying growth stocks.

For better or worse, I passed on each of those trends and other momentum growers as speculation. Instead, I focused on researching and purchasing stocks of boring, out-of-favor, albeit excellent companies outperforming the S&P 500 as a group since the dates I added the representative shares to the portfolio. Wall Street seems to struggle in generating Hamptons beach house-size bonuses on buy-and-hold value investing; instead, it promotes speculative investment trading paradigms producing fees that build those summer cottages. Again, I ask whose beach or lake house are you building—yours or your financial advisor's?

Perhaps there are diverging interpretations of traditional value investing or quality compounders purchased at attractive prices. The trading of value stocks is the equivalent of buying cigar butts or shares of lower-quality companies on speculation, then selling based on an expected or hoped-for corporate, industry, or macro-driven event. In contrast, I will continue to add fresh ideas to my portfolio that offer compelling prospects for compounding capital gains and dividends, protected by adequate margins of safety to preserve principal during the inevitable declines of the market.

Remember, future returns are uncorrelated with past performance. Nonetheless, the objective is to outperform the benchmark over extended periods—seven to ten years or more—knowing monthly, quarterly, and annual performances are at the whim of the market's voting machine cast from irrational investor behavior or the occasional surprise event. It is better to seek the benefits of Graham's longer-tail weighing machine of compounding returns and margins of safety.

Before the COVID-19 coronavirus pandemic, the post-Great Recession bull market—propelled by non-dividend-paying growth, high-yield, cryptocurrency, and other speculative investment strategies—seemed unstoppable. Some market luminaries were questioning the enduring legacy of value investing or outright declared its imminent death. A bull market for the ages precipitated the argument as growth stocks, momentum trading, trend following, and high-yield dividend equity, among other speculative portfolio strategies, were outperforming the more risk-averse value approach.

Perhaps value investing is too long-term and too low-cost for a near-sighted, over-sophisticated financial services industry bent on collecting exorbitant fees and bonuses from its legion of followers. Nevertheless, trying to predict trends, catalysts, and macro events that produce profitable trades with consistency befits a game of chance more than a legitimate professional practice. Despite the noise, value investing triumphs because value does matter in everything we buy, hold, or sell.

Investments in quality, dividend-paying companies at value prices, endure well beyond the scrap heap, where perennial bull markets for the ages dump the portfolios of investors chasing fast money in the euphoria of "This time is different." History argues otherwise.

Value investing is neither dead nor dying and survives as a superior investing strategy. In the post-Great Recession secular bull market, it was camouflaged, with the die-hard practitioners waiting in the bushes ready to pounce on the falling stock prices of enduring enterprises. We are comfortable in acknowledging that value prevails in every market cycle.

The Downside to Value in Extended Bull Markets

The inherent risk to the value investing model is the non-value investors permeating market cycles.

Chasing the dragon named *market bubbles* has been a cornerstone of investing for Wall Street professionals and Main Street do-it-yourselfers since, well, stock trading began. Human behavior dictates that once we outsmart the market and predict this swing or that trend, or go long or short just right on a company or sector, it's off to the races. Convinced of having this thing figured out, we begin the hamster roll of predicting and trading unrestrained.

As validation, there are always reputable assists from outside market influences to our preoccupation with market trends. Of late, there was an assist from the Federal Reserve in keeping interest rates low. Before that, the hand-off came from government deregulation of the housing market, allowing widespread homeownership fueling opportunistic investment banks to package the mortgages into marketable securities, creating more risky mortgage dollars to lend to marginal home buyers.

Before the high-rated—despite no documentation and no income—mortgages, there was an assist from the capital markets of free-flowing investment into dot-com ideas that were just that, ideas. And before that, there was a contribution from junk bonds financing impossible mergers and acquisitions. Yes, the greatest threat to an investor is the market itself; however, the market is also a friend to count on for delivering individual company or market-wide value opportunities. Never knowing when or how those opportunities will emerge, the dedicated value investor stays patient and self-disciplined.

Prepare for the imminent next downturn with dry powder in the form of FDIC-insured cash to ride the ensuing upside in the stocks of quality companies becoming value-priced by the sudden extreme preference for discomfort among the herd of market-timing investors. Rest assured, when market crashes do occur, the speculators with blind faith in trend following, momentum trading, high-yield dividend investing, and the next trading fad yet to be determined will be running for the hills.

As value investors, downturns in the market and at targeted quality enterprises are our workdays. The ensuing upturns are our paydays.

Financial Markets and Farmers' Markets

The proverbial day of reckoning is inevitable, although unpredictable.

The thoughtful value investor never stresses over failed short positions, diminishing fund assets under management from departing performance chasers, or useless self-doubt fueled by the 20/20 hindsight of missing out on the fast growers, high yielders, and Bitcoins when trending skyward. For every speculative winner, such as Amazon, there are several Enrons, Blockbusters, WorldComs, and Lehmann Brothers.

Take extreme comfort in knowing as long as there are financial markets or farmers' markets, value prevails.

Why the Trend Is Never Your Friend

By definition, trend followers pass on the underfollowed player in an underappreciated industry. Nonetheless, following the trend or practicing momentum investing are fleeting, favoring nearsighted, speculative trades that come and go with market cycles and fads.

Common sense suggests that a slew of short-term momentum trades is required to make the same potential profits from just a few long-term investments in the publicly traded shares of quality companies purchased at reasonable prices. The winning long-term holdings were bought at value prices because the traders sold them off during a passing negative trend.

Buy slices of businesses because each appears in demand by the customer yet trades at value prices because of temporary mispricing by the market. Well-managed, concentrated stock portfolios have an adequate allocation of defensive, noncyclical holdings for the eleventh hour of any bull market.

Skeptical, nearsighted investors cite political grandstanding, trade wars, commodity pricing dilemmas, livestock supply issues, occasional product recalls, and other inconsequential grievances as justification for short-sighted momentum trades and trend following. And worse, offer death knell sentiments for companies domiciled outside the US. Being receptive to the compelling counters to an investment thesis, when the value investor hears, "Stay away from car companies," the auto industry becomes a sudden and curious interest.

It is incredible how the investment world, on the whole, believes the present market, whether bull, bear, or range-bound is somehow different, ignoring that business and market cycles come and go at random. Having the newest and latest investment fad to rally around is the differentiator in each market cycle. It reminds me of being in high school all over again.

Take preference for the perception of intrinsic value instead of estimations or calculations. Be skeptical of specific price targets, earnings projections, and other attempts at precision from the sophisticated financial models of sell- and buy-side analysts when attempting to determine the difference between the market price and the underlying value. When you read, "XYZ is trading at a 40 percent discount to intrinsic value," remember how Wall Street justifies enormous fees and bonuses with predictions unnecessary in the scheme of things. If these market pundits were more often right than wrong, we'd become wealthy by just following them. Before taking the prediction at face value, conduct your proper due diligence as outlined in Part II: Strategies.

For example, in mid-2011, the common shares of Microsoft (MSFT) were trading in the low- to mid-twenties. Did I calculate through discounted free cash flow analysis and other complex formulas that Microsoft compounds as a ten-bagger nine years later?

No, although my perception was the market undervalued the stock, in general, despite its Windows software legacy, strong fundamentals, hoards of cash, and other positive areas of the operation. The activist investment community was taking issue with the chief executive officer (CEO) at the time, and I figured at some point, he resigns, retires, or gets replaced. Thus, I invested at a dividend-adjusted $20.87 a share, thinking it is going up more than down over the long-term. My perception was driven by a real-time cognitive analysis more than an assumption-driven specific future price target. As of the June 30, 2020 market close, MSFT was trading at $203 a share, about ten times the cost basis, adjusted for splits and dividends. The holding gained over 725 basis points better than the S&P 500 during the same period.

Over-analysis or setting price targets often gets an individual investor—and perhaps the professional—in trouble from timing trades. The analysis paralysis of publicly traded companies and the underlying stocks leads to extreme shorting or put options trades, as there is bad news to be found in every security.

I am a reformed investor from lessons learned. The slow and steady investor knows that stable companies appreciate in the long run, as the active trader moving in and out of positions in reaction to good and bad news gets punished in the short run. Follow populist stock trends to your potential peril, or invest in a great company over a long-term horizon and benefit from compounding with a margin of safety. The thoughtful, disciplined, and patient investor chases quality and value.

Up next, Part II puts the principles discussed in Part I to work with five proven strategies toward building a portfolio with the potential to outperform the market.

* * *

CHAPTER TEN SUMMARY

On Price and Value

- In the enduring wisdom of super-investor Warren Buffett, price is what you pay; value is what you get. This investment truth was evident throughout Buffett's illustrious career and perhaps will endure forever.

- Value investing was out of favor on Wall Street during the epic post-Great Recession bull market but was reemerging as a result of the COVID-19 coronavirus pandemic. On Main Street, it forever remains an ideal approach to market-beating common stock investing.

- Value investing is never dead; it's just less popular than short-term growth stories.

- Attempts to predict trends, catalysts, momentum, or macro events producing profitable trades with any consistency border on substituting lottery tickets for a retirement plan. Avoid trend following and other investing misdemeanors.

■ The thoughtful, disciplined, and patient investor takes extreme comfort in knowing that as long as there are financial markets and farmers' markets, value prevails.

* * *

PART I: PRINCIPLES

° The principles of *Build Wealth with Common Stocks* are just the tip of the iceberg. What do you practice or want to attempt as a do-it-yourself investor to stay ahead of the market over time?

II

STRATEGIES

Eleven

Define The Value Proposition

H ow well do you know and understand the products or services of
the publicly traded company represented by the shares you own?

Your primary role as a do-it-yourself investor is to uncover the value
proposition of the organization. An enterprise's value proposition is the
sum of the competitive advantages of its products or services in the markets it serves, including the level of attraction of the goods or services to
the customers. In your research, ask the question, "What value do the
products or services offer to existing and potential consumers?"

If you were in the general market for either, would you purchase the
goods or services of the company?

Picture a friend as the managing partner of a similar, although privately held enterprise who invited you to buy in as a partner. Assuming
you had the necessary funds, would you accept the offer?

Your answers to these hypothetical questions validate an understanding and confidence in the prospects of the targeted business from the
value proposition or competitive advantage toward continued growth
and prosperity, as reflected in the stock price over time. The publicly
traded company exhibiting a clear and compelling value proposition is
as coveted as a stock trading at attractive valuation multiples.

This chapter addresses how to define the value proposition of the
products or services of a targeted company and explain it with confidence via an elevator pitch. When researching a stock, at the minimum,
visit the following areas to assess the competitive advantages of the business.

The Intrinsic Value of an SEC Filing

Beyond anything already known about the products or services of the company, the retail investor has a myriad of public information available to vet the value proposition. The most reliable data on hand for the enterprise lies in its filings with the US Securities and Exchange Commission (SEC).

The thoughtful and disciplined investor reads corporate filings with the SEC, such as the 10-K annual reports, 10-Q quarterly reports, and 8-K current events. SEC filings are the primary public resources available for due diligence on the value proposition of the enterprise and its products or services. Access this information on the investor relations section of the company website, at your online broker, or your favorite investment website.

Take the time to delve into the online presence of the organization, including its website, social media presence, plus marketing channels such as advertising, as well as public and investor relations. As the starting point of diligent investment research, reading the Form 10-K report the organization submits to the SEC on an annual basis and reviewing the investor relations site are priorities one and two for the independent investor.

For example, the 10-K, in particular the section titled Item 1 Business, is where management discusses the enterprise with vigor. Topics include background and history of the company, corporate strategy, specific products and services, markets and distribution, competition, supply chains, research and development, intellectual property, foreign and domestic operations, plus other related items specific to the industry. Despite being detailed to the point of sleep-inducing, the information provides a roadmap of the product's or service's potential to propel the stock price upward over a long-term holding period.

The investor website and SEC filings from Apple (AAPL) are among the best prepared and easy to understand of the S&P 500 companies; transparency is often weak and elusive in many enterprises.

I challenge those prone to skip annual reports and other SEC filings to find organizational, product, regulatory, and financial facts about the company you were unaware of before reading. These documents are avalanches of legalese and number crunching. A thorough read often uncovers slices of information that bring you inside—at least on a virtual level—the plants, stores, e-commerce operations, C-suites, and boardrooms.

Competitive Advantages of the Products or Services

A profitable retail common stock portfolio resembles a collection of owned slices of well-managed companies producing in-demand products or services with enduring competitive advantages. Based on the relentless commitment to price and quality, how does the thoughtful investor define the competitive advantages of the product or services offered by the company and the perceived enduring value relative to the market price?

One recommended approach is to gauge how the value proposition of the company rewards each of its stakeholders.

Illustrate the Value Proposition with a Crayon

In *Beating the Street*, Peter Lynch offers an assessment of the importance of understanding what we are investing in without experiencing analysis paralysis: "Never invest in any idea you can't illustrate with a crayon."[1]

The thought came to Lynch after he observed a class of middle school students who formed an investment club under the direction of their teacher. Lynch noted the combined stock picks of the student investment club outperformed the S&P 500 Index by a wide margin. Lynch and his student investors reduced the value proposition to a metaphorical crayon sketch that an investor can understand and communicate with ease.

Can you illustrate the value proposition of the company behind your favorite stock with a crayon, the symbolic equivalent of a short sentence or phrase?

The successful do-it-yourself investor won't buy something because it sounds or feels right; alternatively, allocating hard-earned dollars to the common shares of businesses understood and appreciated. The value proposition is often overlooked or taken for granted by retail investors. At the other extreme, institutional investors, such as portfolio managers and analysts, tend to over-analyze the value proposition of products or services of a targeted company with piles of deep-dive research to justify the fees and bonus structure. The worse investment a stock picker makes is buying the shares of an enterprise despite limited knowledge of what it produces or how it benefits the target market.

The thoughtful, disciplined, and patient investor knows the common stock of a company providing valuable, in-demand products and services endures across market cycles, despite a few erratic price movements in between from the nearsightedness of the crowd, inclusive of individuals and professionals.

The Value Proposition Elevator Pitch

The Model Portfolio holds the common shares of quality enterprises based on a proprietary research model of five fundamentals-driven measurements: shareholder yields, return on management, valuation multiples, downside risk, and the subject of this chapter: the value proposition. Start by attempting to define the competitive advantages of the business in an elevator pitch containing a short sentence or phrase.

Below are the elevator pitches—my investment theses on the value proposition—of the stocks of three companies represented in The Model Portfolio. Please note the overall view reflects each of the primary measures of the proprietary research model as of a June 30, 2020, quarter-end update.

> The Walt Disney Company (DIS) is the undisputed king of media content.

Its in-demand, original content has driven a four-bagger stock since 2009, doubling the two-bagger return of the S&P 500 during the same period. Disney is an outstanding example of the magic of compounding, no pun intended.

> Johnson & Johnson (JNJ) is similar to owning a mutual fund of healthcare products.

Although the talc and opioid lawsuits against J&J were legitimate threats to the stock, the pharmaceutical giant has a history of overcoming adversity.

> Nike, Inc. (NKE): the Swoosh is the moat (competitive advantage).

Phil Knight, the billionaire cofounder of the global apparel powerhouse, paid a graphic design student, attending a college where he taught accounting courses, $35 for creating the now-famous logo for his athletic footwear start-up. Rest assured, Nike later compensated her with a generous stock option grant.[2] Great businesses are successful, in large part, from taking care of stakeholders.

The Crowd Buys What Sounds or Feels Good

Grasping the value proposition of a publicly traded company, such as reflected in its products or services, is crucial to the fundamental analysis of the targeted shares of common stocks for the retail investor to buy and hold and take advantage of compounding total return. Start with the 10-K annual report to gain knowledge of the products or services as well as the employees, suppliers, markets, governments, and customers producing, trading, regulating, and consuming the goods or services.

Next, attempt to define the value proposition of the offerings from the enterprise in a short phrase or elevator pitch. If you are comfortable with a basic understanding of the business, continue your due diligence toward possible ownership of a slice of the company via its common shares.

When struggling to define and explain the value proposition in the form of an elevator pitch, or—borrowing the metaphor of Peter Lynch's market-beating investment club of seventh-graders—with a crayon, it is perhaps advisable to move on to the next idea. Too many crowdsourced investors buy and sell shares based on market sentiment, trends, and fads without understanding the value proposition of the company represented by the underlying stock.

Begin with the Value Proposition in Mind

Understanding the products or services and the competitive advantages of the targeted company is paramount to the thriving retail investor. To own a business, we must acquaint ourselves with the enterprise generating the numbers that constitute the equity analysis. The crowd pays less attention to the intangibles of the business and focuses on overanalyzing the more tangible metrics. The more you know about the companies you invest in, the higher the potential for your portfolio to outperform. If a friend or loved one asked you to invest in a yet unpatented invention of some crazy virtual reality science fiction game based on a crude drawing and a just minted engineering degree, would you?

Notwithstanding the alluring power of love and friendship, you perhaps invest little, if any, of your hard-earned dollars. Instead, own companies whose goods or services are understood in principle, whether you use any of the products. Begin your research by attempting to define the value proposition. If you cannot explain it or are suspect of any clear and concise competitive advantages, save your precious time and dry powder for a better opportunity.

Up next: Chapter Twelve explores the strategy of quantifying shareholder yields.

* * *

CHAPTER ELEVEN SUMMARY

On Competitive Advantages

- The value proposition of a publicly traded company is the sum of the competitive advantages of its products and services in the markets it serves.

- In researching a targeted stock, it is crucial to uncover the value proposition of the business before taking an ownership slice.

- Read the filings submitted by senior management to the Securities and Exchange Commission (SEC), such as the 10-K annual reports, 10-Q quarterly reports, and 8-K current events.

- When unable to define or understand the value proposition of the enterprise, consider taking a pass on the stock.

- Understanding the products or services and competitive advantages with conviction is essential to the thriving retail common stock investor.

Twelve

Quantify Shareholder Yields

When researching a stock for inclusion in The Model Portfolio, I consider the returns to shareholders a leading barometer of the worthiness of owning a slice of the business. The thoughtful, retail-level investor quantifies shareholder yields beyond just dividends. As does Warren Buffett, view the shareholder yields of a stock as the equivalent of its equity bond rate.

A simple definition of the equity bond rate is how the returns on the company and the underlying stock compare to those of government-issued bonds. Dividend yields are the typical comparable, but consider two other metrics to quantify the actual return to shareholders. Measure the average of the sum of yields per share on trailing earnings and free cash flow, in addition to the dividend.

Next, weigh the sum against the prevailing Ten-Year Treasury rate. This proprietary equity bond rate modeling gives you a sense of whether a stock is worthy of the assumed higher-risk profile compared to the perceived safer intermediate-term government issue.

Implement this methodology to confirm the shareholder yields of your targeted stock are exceeding the Ten-Year Treasury rate. Despite being out of favor on Wall Street, seek publicly traded companies generating multiple, Treasury-beating shareholder yields.

This chapter introduces an alternative yield methodology toward outperforming Treasury rates without the limitations of the dividend growth strategy—such as overweighting dividend history—or the risks of high-yield dividend investing.

Earnings Yield

The earnings yield (EY) is the annualized trailing earnings per share (EPS) divided by the stock's closing price. Earnings yield is the inverse of the price-to-earnings ratio (P/E) and measured in a more usable percentage format than the P/E multiple by providing a comparable yield profile to a bond rate. The EPS represents the portion of profits allocated to each outstanding share of common stock. Earnings yield is an indicator of how the company's earnings per common share are relative to the stock price. A higher EY indicates more robust earnings per dollar invested.

When comparing stocks to prevailing bond rates, the earnings yield provides a more accurate measure than the dividend yield. Boards raise and lower dividend payouts at will. Besides, non-dividend-paying stocks also generate earnings yields.

Look for stocks with earnings yields of at least 300 to 400 basis points—3 to 4 percentage points—above the Ten-Year Treasury yield. Targeting earnings yields above 6 percent is the equivalent of price-to-earnings ratios below 17 times.

The higher the earnings yield and thus, the lower the P/E ratio, the more unfavorable the stock appears to the market. Nevertheless, as value investors, quality enterprises with high earnings yields grab our attention for further research. The historic bull market that occurred during the writing of this book favored stocks over treasuries; however, earnings yield becomes a reliable barometer of whether to favor common stocks over government bonds in any market cycle.

Earnings yield is a leading margin of safety indicator of The Model Portfolio.

Free Cash Flow Yield

Free cash flow yield (FCFY) shows how much a business generates in free cash flow each year per common share relative to the stock price. Hence, free cash flow yield is trailing free cash flow per share divided by the closing stock price. Free cash flow is income after taxes minus preferred dividends plus depreciation, depletion, and amortization expense net of capital expenditures. It is more indicative of the bottom line of a company than is net profit.

Free cash flow allows senior management to enhance shareholder value by pursuing capital deployment opportunities such as research and development, mergers and acquisitions, dividend payments, share repurchases, and debt reduction.

Some investors trust free cash flow over earnings because of the GAAP/non-GAAP—the acronym for generally accepted accounting principles—controversy surrounding earnings calculations. Analyze the returns for both as having more information about a company and the underlying stock is to your advantage. Nonetheless, keep in mind that free cash flow represents a byproduct of earnings. The Model Portfolio stock screen presented in Part III, Chapter Sixteen, looks for a free cash flow yield above 7 percent, an ideal target signaling a free cash flow multiple of fewer than fifteen times.

Earnings quality is also measured by cash flow margin (CFM) or operating cash flow divided by trailing sales. Operating cash flow is income after taxes minus preferred dividends and other distributions, plus depreciation, depletion, and amortization expense. Favor cash flow margins that are above 10 percent. Think of CFM as a flash indicator of the vertical cash flow management by senior executives.

Cash hoard per share or the amount of cash on hand plus any short and liquid long-term investments on the balance sheet divided by common shares outstanding has been newsworthy in recent years. In simple terms, by subtracting cash per share from the stock price, an investor gets a more definitive representation of the enterprise's intrinsic value, net of cash and investments. Indeed, an insignificant spread between the two prices presents an alluring investment opportunity. Cash hoard provides senior management with hedges during economic downturns, interest-free financing for strategic acquisitions, and redistribution of capital to shareholders via stock buybacks or increased dividends.

Free cash flow yield is a leading profitability indicator of The Model Portfolio.

Dividend Yield

Target companies with a dividend yield or the annual dividend rate divided by the current stock price exceeding 2 percent and below 6 percent; however, buy the dividend-paying stock of a quality company trading at an attractive price if the historical yield is below 2 percent. Trailing dividend yield indicates how much a company paid out in dividends for the previous twelve months relative to the share price. The dividend rate is the dollar sum of dividends paid over the prior fiscal year.

A value investor, somewhat in contrast to a dividend growth investor, looks for dividends to keep paid in the short-term while waiting for the investment thesis and capital appreciation to play out over time. And, unlike the growth investor, places less emphasis on trailing and projected dividend payouts. As highlighted in Part I: Chapter Nine, avoid stocks with payout ratios or the percentage of net income allocated to dividends exceeding 60 percent.

Average the Sum of Total Yields

Now, average the earnings, free cash flow, and dividend yields per share. Averaging the yields on trailing earnings, free cash flow, and dividends provides a snapshot of the performance of the stock against the benchmark Treasury rate. The Ten-Year Treasury yield is the published rate on the prevailing Ten-Year Treasury benchmark note.

Shareholder Yields Rating

The resulting shareholder yield rating is bullish if well above the Ten-Year Treasury rate, neutral if in the same range, or bearish if below the rate based on the average of total yields of the stock.

The Model Portfolio considers shareholder yields of a publicly traded stock as a leading barometer of the worthiness of owning a slice of the business.

Four Stocks Generating High Shareholder Yields

Based on the sentiment meters of short interest—the number or percentage of shares borrowed and sold short by investors who consider the stock overvalued—price performance versus the S&P 500 benchmark, and attractive valuation multiples, four of my favorite companies were out of favor on Wall Street.

Here are the picks from The Model Portfolio, including an elevator pitch for each company as of the period ending June 30, 2020. Each stock was yielding more than seven times the prevailing Ten-Year Treasury rate after averaging the three metrics of earnings yield, free cash flow yield, and dividend yield.

Company (Ticker):	Comcast (CMCSA)	CVS Health (CVS)	Kroger (KR)	Southwest Airlines (LUV)
EPS Yield	6.46%	8.50%	7.77%	11.85%
FCF Yield	6.67%	13.81%	13.91%	15.39%
Dividend Yield	2.21%	3.07%	1.88%	2.21%
Average Yield	**5.11%**	**8.46%**	**7.85%**	**9.82%**
Treasury Rate	0.66%	0.66%	0.66%	0.66%

Exceptional Shareholder Yields
Source: The Model Portfolio at davidjwaldron.com. Data as of June 30, 2020.

Table Key

- EPS Yield — earnings yield or twelve-month trailing GAAP earnings per share divided by closing share price (CSP).
- FCF Yield — free cash flow yield or twelve-month trailing free cash flow per share divided by CSP.
- Dividend Yield — trailing full-year dividend rate divided by CSP.
- Average Yield — the average of the earnings, free cash flow, and dividend yields.
- Treasury Rate — the prevailing US Ten-Year Treasury yield as of June 30, 2020.

Value Proposition Elevator Pitch for Each Pick

- Comcast (CMCSA) is the queen of content and king of delivery.

- CVS Health (CVS) is the one-stop health store for medical insurance, primary care, and prescriptions.

- Kroger (KR) is the originator of the supermarket model and a defensive stock.

- Southwest Airlines (LUV) is the ever-profitable leader in airline discounting — pandemics notwithstanding.

As expected, professional traders and panicky retail investors got caught up in the projected impact of the COVID-19 coronavirus pandemic event on CMCSA, CVS, KR, and LUV, slamming each stock price with share dumps or short positions. On the contrary, I reason that in the long-term, the share prices of Treasury-beating, well-run companies are destined to outperform.

A Balanced Approach to Value-Based Investing

Earnings per share are controversial because of creative financial engineering by company executives. Free cash flow, or the net cash available after capital expenditures and other asset costs, is a more precise measurement of the real net earnings after income taxes and capital investment. Nevertheless, earnings and cash flow yields are the foremost valuation tools for measuring the market sentiment on a business based on the relationship of its bottom line to the stock price.

Most high-yield and some dividend growth investors gravitate to dividend yields far exceeding the Ten-Year Treasury rate. On the contrary, the disciplined investor is cautious with dividends susceptible to erratic stock price fluctuations, unexpected rate decreases, or unsustainable payout ratios.

The dividend payout from an expensive stock equates to a dividend purchased or held at a high cost. Value and price prevail in every area of investing. Thus, practice the more balanced approach of value-based buy-and-hold total-return investing.

Quantify Shareholder Yields Beyond the Dividend

The thoughtful retail-level investor quantifies shareholder yields beyond the more conventional dividend payout.

When investing in the stocks of non-dividend-paying companies, earnings and free cash flow yields are telling valuation alternatives. Nonetheless, as a shareholder, you deserve a compounding return or yield from each leg of the earnings vertical, dividends included.

If the shareholder yields are underperforming the ten-year government bond benchmark, consider the company unworthy of taking an ownership slice because of the higher equity risk. The thoughtful investor deems a stock as unattractive when shareholder yields are inferior to holding a Treasury bond or note backed by the alleged full faith and credit of the US government.

My proprietary approach to measuring the equity bond rate is one example. Also, think about what you are attempting to uncover as a do-it-yourself investor in fostering confidence that a targeted common stock has the potential to be more valuable than a conventional government bond over a long-term holding period.

In contrast to fixed-income investors, the dedicated common stock investor avoids lending money to companies as a bondholder. Some gentlemen and gentlewomen prefer bonds, although the thoughtful investor favors the multiple shareholder yields of equities.

CHAPTER TWELVE SUMMARY

On Shareholder Returns

- The returns to shareholders by a publicly traded company are a leading barometer of the worthiness of owning a slice of the business.

- As a shareholder, you deserve a compounding return or yield from each leg of the earnings vertical.

- Average the earnings, free cash flow, and dividend yields and compare to the Ten-Year Treasury rate in determining the equity bond rate of the individual stock.

- Common shares underperforming the Ten-Year Treasury become unworthy candidates for the thoughtful buy-and-hold investor.

- What other areas do you examine to determine if a targeted common stock has the potential to be more valuable than a conventional government bond over an extended holding period?

Thirteen

Measure The Return On Management

I have modeled and implemented five fundamentals areas of investment research toward building a market-beating family portfolio for eleven years running: value proposition, shareholder yields, valuation multiples, downside risk, and in this chapter, return on management.

Although advisable to focus on the business's fundamental structure, it is the senior management, in partnership with the board of directors and the employees, who are producing and delivering the goods and services.

By keeping investment research focused on a few crucial metrics combined with a pinch of common sense, the disciplined investor has the potential to outperform sophisticated deep-dive analyses and achieve alpha with lower costs and less risk, despite any capital limitations. This chapter covers prime examples of C-suite-driven metrics of a publicly traded company to analyze toward measuring the return on management.

Evaluate Management Effectiveness

Understanding the performance of senior management is paramount to owning slices of excellent companies. When considering the worthiness of inclusion in your portfolio, examine the actual growth metrics of the company as opposed to speculative forecasts of what might occur with future revenues, earnings per share, free cash flow or dividend growth.

Seek cash-generating companies providing wide, or at least comfortable, margins of safety. Favor businesses with efficient and transparent management leveraging returns for customers, employees, and shareholders.

Future price targets and other exacting projections are unreliable and best left to market speculators. Only a select few metrics are necessary to determine management effectiveness toward the potential for market-beating performance.

The challenge of evaluating management is the propensity to discover inadequacies or even questionable behavior. If conducting audits of businesses whose shares we own or products and services we buy to eliminate what misaligns with our beliefs and values, we end up managing a light portfolio within a bare-bones lifestyle. Thus, a laser focus on the management-driven fundamentals of chosen businesses best serves the retail investor.

Companies with robust fundamentals producing quality, in-demand products or services are the foundation of a market-beating portfolio; however, you are investing in its human resources as much as the assets and liabilities listed on the balance sheet. Nevertheless, quality companies endure, regardless of the leadership at any given time.

Growth in Revenue, Earnings, and Dividends

Remember to seek companies already growing, regardless of any promises for growth. Evaluate a minimum of three-year trailing growth in revenue or the compounded annual growth rate of net sales.

In addition to revenue growth, look at three-year earnings per share and dividend growth as key indicators of the fundamental strength of the company and the commitment to increasing the wealth shared with its owners. Whether measuring growth, earnings, or dividends, sift for double-digit—or at least positive—compounded annualized growth rates (CAGR).

As of the period ending June 30, 2020, the holdings in The Model Portfolio had a cumulative average three-year revenue growth of 7.65

percent. Top-line growth is the primary measure of the potential endurance of an enterprise.

Operating and Net Profit Margins

Is the company profitable?

Only speculators and misinformed investors go long the stock of a company losing money. A no-brainer rule of retail-level investing is if you want never to lose money, avoid taking long positions in businesses that are unprofitable. Instead, take a look at the trailing twelve-month operating margin—EBIT, or earnings before interest and taxes, divided by revenue—and net profit margin, or the trailing twelve months of income after taxes divided by sales. Net profit margin is the percent of revenues remaining after paying operating expenses, interest, and income taxes for the trailing twelve months, or TTM, divided by trailing sales, also referred to as NOPAT — net operating profit after taxes.*

Again, favor double-digit top- and bottom-line margins or at least superior growth for companies within industries where single-digit margins are the norm. Although somewhat rare for large-cap companies, always be on the lookout for double-digit profit margins providing cushions against downward macro and microeconomic cycles.

As of the quarter ending June 30, 2020, the constituent companies in The Model Portfolio had a cumulative average net profit margin of 12.72 percent.

* * *

*Note: It is unnecessary to get caught up in the math of these complex formulas, as most online brokers and investment websites provide the calculations to the end user at no cost.

Return on Equity

The return on equity (ROE), or how well the company generates net income as a percentage of the total net investment in the stock, is another reliable measure of management effectiveness. Return on equity is trailing income available to common shareholders divided by average stockholders' equity from the most recent fiscal year (MRFY) and the year-earlier fiscal period, expressed as a percentage. Return on equity reveals how much profit a business generates from shareholder investment in the stock.

Seek a minimum ROE of 15 percent. As of the quarter ending on June 30, 2020, about two-thirds of the holdings in The Model Portfolio were exceeding the 15 percent target, with a cumulative average return on equity of 28.80 percent, almost double the ROE threshold. Nonetheless, be aware of senior management using aggressive stock buybacks to inflate the return on equity. On the contrary, if executed by the board of directors with sound strategy and at bargain prices, stock repurchases provide a value-add to shareholders of record.

In mergers and acquisitions, companies more often commit the same malpractice as individual investors by overpaying for shares of stock. Boards sometimes overpay for shares when doing buybacks as well.

Return on Invested Capital

To see how much a company is earning on the capital it deploys from operations, Benjamin Graham taught his students to look beyond EPS to return on invested capital. ROIC is net income after taxes divided by the average of total equity plus the sum of total long-term debt, total other liabilities, deferred income tax, and minority interest, expressed as a percentage.

Like Graham and Warren Buffett, place a premium on the return on invested capital or how well a company is allocating its financial resources to generate incremental profits for the business. Target companies that are producing an ROIC of 12 percent or higher.

The return on invested capital is only as reliable as the underlying weighted average cost of the capital (WACC). The weighted average cost of capital weighs each category of financial resources in proportion. Sources of capital, including common stock, preferred stock, bonds, and any other long-term debt, are included in a WACC calculation. The weighted average cost of capital is the estimated outlay of those resources before returns and, thus, reduces net income.

Return on invested capital demonstrates the ability of management to outperform its capital costs. Thus, an investor needs to confirm the ROIC exceeds the WACC by a comfortable margin. Return on invested capital, as it relates to WACC, presents a primary measure of the potential for the enterprise to provide a compounding annual return on the stock price over long periods. When the ROIC diminishes toward the underlying cost of capital, the business faces the inverse threat of a decrease in valuation and an increase in risk.

As of the quarter ending June 30, 2020, The Model Portfolio had a cumulative average ROIC of 10.75 percent against a WACC of 4.88 percent. The overall ROIC was below the 12 percent target and had experienced a significant drop from 22.59 percent before the COVID-19 event. The constituent companies, on average, were deploying capital at over four times its cost before the 2020 second quarter fall-out in fundamentals, market-wide.

Return on invested capital is a leading fundamentals and margin of safety indicator of The Model Portfolio.

Remember the Internal Customer

A unique approach of the thoughtful investor is the measurement of employee satisfaction, including the evaluation of the CEO by the rank and file. Although gathered from nonscientific data of the all-too-biased internet, a snapshot look at employee morale quantifies the cultural dynamic of the organization.

Job search sites such as Glassdoor and Indeed are ideal places to start evaluating employee reviews, including CEO ratings. Employee reviews and the rankings of the CEO of an established company are often intertwined. Everything starts with leadership. The respect for a CEO shown by those working within the same culture has the propensity to move the needle. It takes a village to shift an organization north or south.

Satisfied employees are inclined to deliver quality products and excellent service, translating to loyal customers and sustainable profitability. A dominant market share held by a significant player within an industry attracts faithful customers no matter the level of employee morale or CEO popularity. Nevertheless, poor-performing CEOs produce value opportunities. Own the common shares of wonderful companies trading at sensible prices, no matter the chief at the time of purchase.

Remember to seek high-quality companies with attractive long-term prospects, knowing the potential for compounding total return on capital and dividends increases when the stock exhibits a margin of safety at purchase. The enduring quality of the operator remains paramount to the success of the investment over time.

The proverbial chicken and egg question begs, *What comes first, a quality company or competent management?*

Senior executives and board members come and go; therefore, it is imperative to own stock in companies that demonstrate enduring quality operations with an outstanding overall return on management despite the inevitable turnover. And when the occasional and unintentional misfire hire is the newest member of the C-suite, resist pressing the panic button. Sit back and watch as the market sends in the prowling bears. Next, take advantage of the sudden out-of-favor enterprise as an opportunity to buy more shares of a persistent quality business at temporary bargain prices.

Management Rating

After measuring growth, profitability, capital allocation, return on equity, and other barometers of management effectiveness, assign a management rating to the stock: bullish, neutral, or bearish based on your weighting of the overall return on management.

Invest in the Executive's EQ

Numerous studies and books have argued that in everyday life, so-called emotional intelligence (EQ) outperforms the more understood intelligence quotient (IQ). In my observations, the emotional intelligence of an executive is more apt to produce profitable outcomes than a high IQ seasoned with an Ivy League MBA.

Emotional intelligence is the capability of individuals to have an awareness of the emotions of self and those of others, discerning between the different feelings and addressing each as appropriate. Productive individuals use sensory information to guide thinking and behavior, and manage or adjust emotions to adapt to environments or achieve goals.

The same holds for corporate management. Similar to Wall Street institutions, high IQs supported by MBAs from prominent universities are often a prerequisite for entry to the C-suite of corporate America. Nonetheless, EQ is perhaps the driving force behind successful managers, regardless of IQ or alma mater. In his groundbreaking book *Good to Great*, Jim Collins referred to a business leader with high emotional intelligence as a "Level 5 executive who builds enduring greatness through a paradoxical blend of personal humility and professional will."[1]

As a former executive, I observed leaders with high EQs and Level 5 leadership abilities—humbled but driven—seemed to outperform peers relying on high IQs, unique talents, or charisma. The rare manager with both a high IQ and EQ has first inherited and further developed the gifts to achieve legendary status. Think Warren Buffett at Berkshire

Hathaway, Tim Cook of Apple, Satya Nadella at Microsoft, and Bob Iger of Disney.

Companies with Notable Returns on Management

To demonstrate the importance of strong leadership, The Model Portfolio holds select companies exhibiting exceptional returns on management. The next table depicts the management effectiveness metrics of five companies in the portfolio at the time of this writing: Apple (AAPL), Microsoft (MSFT), Nike (NKE), TJX Companies (TJX), and Union Pacific (UNP).

As of the quarter ending June 30, 2020, each representative company was performing with positive three-year revenue growth, double-digit profit margins—high single digits for retailer TJX—and generating outstanding returns on equity and invested capital. Plus, the sample companies had positive total returns since inception, each outperforming the overall gains of the S&P 500 during the same holding period.

All figures other than dates are percentage returns.

Holding	AAPL	MSFT	NKE	TJX	UNP
Revenue Growth	12.60	12.60	9.20	10.80	8.80
Net Profit Margin	21.35	33.36	10.46	7.48	27.85
Return on Equity	62.09	43.82	47.35	60.65	34.08
Return on Capital	22.56	28.88	16.20	10.15	11.01
One-Year Return	84.32	51.92	16.80	(4.39)	(0.02)
S&P 500 Return	5.39	5.39	5.39	5.39	5.39
Date Added	3/10/17	6/28/11	6/15/17	5/23/17	8/9/10
Total Return	174.66	875.13	91.73	42.22	477.82
S&P Total Return	30.67	139.10	64.27	29.26	174.90

Notable Returns on Management
Source: The Model Portfolio at davidjwaldron.com. Note: Calculations are percentages (%)
for the period ending June 30, 2020.

Table Key

- ○ Revenue Growth — revenue growth percentage for the trailing three years.
- ○ Net Profit Margin — net operating profit after taxes as a percentage of net revenue for the trailing twelve months.
- ○ Return on Equity — return on equity percentage annualized from the most recent fiscal year.
- ○ Return on Capital — return on invested capital percentage annualized from the most recent fiscal year.
- ○ One-Year Return — one-year total-return (or loss) percentage of the performance of the stock adjusted for splits and dividends.
- ○ S&P 500 Return — one-year percentage performance of the index adjusted for dividends.
- ○ Date Added — calendar date of the stock's entry to The Model Portfolio.
- ○ Total Return — return performance of the stock adjusted for splits and dividends since the date added to the portfolio.
- ○ S&P Total Return — total return performance of the S&P 500 Index since the date the portfolio added the corresponding stock.

By focusing on the fundamentals that matter without regard to the institutional pressures of fast-money-seeking clients and quarterly out-of-the-park performance, the thoughtful, disciplined, and patient individual investor increases the likelihood of market-beating returns. The cumulative total return outperformance of the benchmark by these select companies in The Model Portfolio reminds us that beating the market is possible over a long-term holding period.

The preceding table ignores the investing strategies of value proposition, shareholder returns, valuation multiples, or downside risk of the five listed companies. Readers need to conduct further due diligence as the measurement of management performance is just one part of the overall proprietary fundamentals analysis of *Build Wealth with Common Stocks*.

Numbers Don't Lie — Whereas Humans Do

When a company misses or beats the Wall Street sell-side analysts' earnings estimates, the question arises, *Who are the actual winners and losers: the management or the analysts?*

An alien investor observing from Mars is scratching its head at how the investing universe on Earth reacts to earnings releases with frantic buying and selling, confirmation-biased bearish and bullish arguments, and predictions of where the company and the stock are heading, with conviction, no less. Such mayhem compels any outsider to short the shares of the publicly traded Wall Street investment firms missing the estimates, never mind the targeted company.

Contrary to the proverbial Wall Street quarterly competition of win, lose, or draw, it becomes more believable if senior management missed or beat its guidance despite any inherent ability to manipulate the forecast. Nevertheless, a tongue-in-cheek favorite earnings headline is XYZ beats by $.01. The one penny wins remind investors that numbers are incapable of lying, although the individuals driving and crunching them forever hold the capacity to finagle. Senior executives of varying qualities are sure to come and go and when least expected. Therefore, stick with companies that hold enduring value.

Measuring actual return on management compels the thoughtful, disciplined, and patient investor to limit precious capital to the stocks of quality operators held for the long-term to profit from the compounding returns courtesy of superior capital allocators.

* * *

CHAPTER THIRTEEN SUMMARY

On Management Effectiveness

- It is essential to investigate how the senior management of the company, in partnership with the board of directors, employees, vendors, and suppliers, are producing and delivering their goods or services.

■ You are investing in a company's human resources as much as the assets and liabilities listed on the balance sheet.

■ At a minimum, measure the senior management returns on growth, profitability, equity, and capital.

■ Include the internal customer in your research, as happy employees are inclined to deliver quality products and excellent services, translating to loyal customers and sustainable profit margins.

■ By focusing on key business fundamentals without regard to the institutional investor pressures of fast-money-seeking clients demanding quarter-by-quarter, out-of-the-park performance or bust, you increase the potential to produce market-beating returns on your common stock holdings.

Fourteen

Weigh Valuation Multiples

A primary tenet of searching for stock investing nirvana or alpha is determining the attractiveness of a stock price based on valuation multiples relative to the fundamentals.

As an individual investor on Main Street, uncover asymmetric price/value opportunities without the need for the typical Wall Street prerequisites by targeting your due diligence on five key fundamental strategic areas of the business highlighted in this part of the book. Then, add a pinch of common sense.

This chapter focuses on valuation multiples—including preferred ratios—plus five undervalued stocks of quality companies in The Model Portfolio discovered using this proprietary valuation matrix.

The Quality + Value Strategy

Some market pundits believe in predicting future price movements with abandon. The proverbial crystal ball—disguised in the sophisticated clothing of technical charts, trends, and assumptions—wreaks havoc on the portfolios of unsuspecting investors modeling speculative market plays. The disciplined value investor never attempts to predict an exact stock price or the percentage changes, whether one, three, or five years from now, never mind next week.

For the value-based investor, an alluring stock price becomes a non-negotiable prerequisite to initiating the productive partial ownership of a quality company. And the preservation of capital becomes supreme following the stock purchase.

In a mission to keep investing super simple, I rely on just four multiples serving as indicators or measurements of the potential mispricing of the stock: revenue, earnings, cash flow, and market sentiment. For entertainment, the chapter also peeks at a few other more speculative multiples. In the recent volatile, albeit cash-rich, tax- and interest rate-advantaged US stock market, companies with generous shareholder yields and high capital allocations from management were commonplace. Nonetheless, finding quality operators with compelling valuations was challenging.

A fundamental premise of this book is the potential for increasing annualized compounding from total return on capital and dividends improves when purchasing common shares with wide margins of safety. The savvy retail investor seeks a price point below the general estimate of the intrinsic value of the company, as represented by the underlying stock.

An investor contemplating what the specific stock price is going to be at any given time in the future can save face and instead buy or sell speculative and risky options and futures; however, as with any casino, good luck with those house-advantaged games. Again, the disciplined stock investor on Main Street refuses to interpret the Wall Street consensus as a definitive buy or sell signal. Evaluating the sentiment on a stock is entertaining, although an earnest dive into a contrarian's treasure trove.

Introduced in Part I: Chapter Three, a confident calculation of margin of safety provides a useful measure of the intrinsic worth of a company based on recent or trailing indices as opposed to assumptive future cash flows and other crystal ball projections. Thus, measure the margin of safety of a targeted holding for longer-term value investing as opposed to shorter-term value trading.

Is It Sinful to Wish for a Market Correction?

The thoughtful investor follows the glorified quarterly Wall Street game of hit or miss for the sole purpose of discovering valuation opportunities in the stocks of quality companies. To paraphrase Warren Buffett, 'the overactive investors on Wall Street are serving the patient investors on Main Street.'

The conscientious investor never wishes for a macro or microeconomic event resulting in negative consequences for jobs and portfolios. When one occurs, the available dry powder gets allocated to the discounted stock prices of quality companies that often ensue. One cannot change history, just one's reaction to it. Stick to the basic tenet of the value-based investor's search for alpha by focusing on the attractiveness of a stock based on valuation metrics relative to the underlying fundamentals of the business.

Market Consensus

The market consensus is the estimate of the combined unanimity on a stock by analysts, bloggers, portfolio managers, retail investors, and employees or internal customers. The contrarian assumes the crowd is wrong in context to the longer-term prospects of the company. Although additional research is necessary to confirm or contradict the accord, the consensus is often a counterintuitive indicator for the thoughtful investor.

Preferred Intrinsic Value Indicators

The Model Portfolio contains companies trading on major US exchanges—none are over-the-counter issues—meeting initial quality tests such as a competitive value proposition, shareholder friendliness, management effectiveness, and acceptable levels of downside risk. Just as important, at the time of purchase, these stocks were trading at sensible prices per the preferred valuation multiples. Tickers held in the portfolio or on the watchlist are subject to further research to verify which companies, if any, are worthy of initial or continued partial ownership.

Think of an investment strategy that combines quality and value as the best opportunity to generate compounding total return over an extended holding period. Here are the preferred valuation multiples used to build and monitor The Model Portfolio.

Price to Sales

The price-to-sales (P/S) ratio measures the stock price relative to revenue. Price-to-sales is the previous market day closing price divided by the sum of sales per share over the trailing twelve months (TTM). Interpret two times or below as an attractive multiple—or at least below the industry average—when measuring a stock price relative to its revenue stream.

As a former executive, I have long held that improved revenue often solves the financial problems a business may be experiencing. When the market underestimates net revenues in the context of the stock price, a potential buying opportunity for a quality operator presents itself. The price-to-sales ratio is perhaps the best barometer of intrinsic value because revenue drives earnings. Earnings are subject to accounting rules and massaging by management; revenue less so, and thus, justify a more substantial weighting of the P/S, including a comparison to the industry peers of the targeted company.

Price-to-sales is a leading valuation indicator of The Model Portfolio.

Price to Trailing Earnings

The price-to-trailing earnings (P/E) ratio is the perennial valuation multiple in the investing universe. Price-to-earnings is the closing stock price divided by the sum of GAAP diluted earnings per share (EPS) over the trailing twelve months (TTM). As a reminder, GAAP is the acronym for generally accepted accounting principles. As discussed in Chapter

Twelve, the inverse of P/E or earnings yield—trailing earnings per share divided by the stock price—quantifies the equity bond rate of the stock as compared to the US Ten-Year Treasury note.

Of the four preferred multiples used in The Model Portfolio, I place the least weight on the P/E ratio when estimating the intrinsic value of a stock price.

Price to Operating Cash Flow

Value investors are frequent interpreters of favorable cash flow multiples as a leading intrinsic value indicator. The price-to-operating cash flow (P/CF) ratio is the closing stock price divided by cash flow per share for the most recent fiscal year. Measuring cash flow multiples provides a reliable interpretation of the intrinsic value of a stock price. For the best value, look for stocks trading at a single-digit multiple to the operating cash flow, or at least below the sector or industry average.

Operating cash flow represents the cash available from net income. Keep in mind that per accounting rules, operating cash flow is higher, equal, or lower than net income based on the allowable adjustments used by senior management.

Investors also use price-to-free cash flow (P/FCF) when weighing valuation multiples. Introduced in Chapter Twelve, free cash flow is operating cash flow after capital expenditures. Price to cash flow is more reliable than P/FCF because of the subjective interpretation of free cash flow. Use the operating cash flow for the sake of consistency as well as availability. Nevertheless, cash is king—or queen—and whenever the market discounts cash flow in the stock price of a quality operator, take notice.

As a net product of the earnings vertical, cash flow acts as a more reliable indicator of value in the context of earnings quality than earnings per share. If P/E is the big picture, then P/CF is the nuts and bolts of the earnings quality of the company in the framework of market sentiment on its ability to convert profits into free cash flow for investment and working capital.

Price-to-operating-cash flow is a leading valuation indicator of The Model Portfolio.

Enterprise Value to Operating Earnings

Enterprise-value-to-operating earnings (EV/EBITDA) is market capitalization plus debt, minority interest, and preferred shares, minus total cash and cash equivalents (EV) divided by operating earnings or earnings before interest, taxes, depreciation, and amortization (EBITDA). How does the operating profit of the company align with market-wide investor interest in the stock?

Screen for stocks appearing undervalued in the context of the operating earnings of the corporation. In general, fewer than 12 times EV/EBITDA reflects an attractive stock price. EV/EBITDA offers a useful contrarian sentiment indicator of whether the crowd has overbought a stock as indicated by the higher multiple or oversold shares as reflected in the lower multiple.

Investing is about the earnings, and the market tends to either pay fair market value or overpay. On occasion, the speculators and algorithms sparked by news, rumors, quarterly reports, or other short-term catalysts create a rare opportunity when the stock of a quality operator gets oversold.

An investor gains a good measure of market sentiment on a stock by evaluating the enterprise value to operating earnings. The value investor paying attention pounces on the sudden marked-down equity merchandise waiting in the financial shopping cart, whether buying off a watchlist or adding additional shares to a portfolio holding.

Enterprise-value-to-operating earnings is a leading valuation indicator of The Model Portfolio.

Valuation Rating

Rate a stock that you have researched for valuation as bullish, neutral, or bearish based on the weighting of the four preferred valuation multiples of the common shares on the whole.

Frustrating as it is, owned equities held in a portfolio or targeted common shares on a watchlist more often appear at fair value or overvalued to the investor focused on owning the mispriced stocks of quality companies over long-term holding periods. Practice discipline and patience to keep sifting for value with regularity; the occasional surprise bargain often appears when least expected.

Five Quality Stocks Trading at Attractive Multiples

The Model Portfolio had five examples of select dividend-paying stocks of profitable, quality companies with compelling value propositions, shareholder yields far exceeding the Ten-Year Treasury rate, and trading at appealing valuation multiples. Comcast (CMCSA), CVS Health (CVS), Kroger (KR), Southwest Airlines (LUV), and Toyota Motor (TM).

The following table illustrates the price-to-sales, earnings, operating cash flow, and enterprise value for each stock at the June 30, 2020, quarter-end update of The Model Portfolio (MP). Also included are the targeted multiples discussed in this chapter and the cumulative average valuation multiples for the portfolio on the whole during the same period.

Remember to conduct your due diligence or consult a licensed broker or registered investment advisor before investing in these or any equities.

* * *

Ticker	CMCSA	CVS	KR	LUV	TM	Target	MP
P/S	1.65	0.32	0.20	0.83	0.62	<2.00	2.84
P/E	15.47	11.77	12.99	10.04	7.38	<17.00	22.39
P/CF	7.41x	5.99	4.03	7.32	4.90	<10.00	18.70
EV/OE	8.37	9.61	6.60	5.78	7.02	<12.00	14.30

Five Examples of Attractive Valuation Multiples
Source: The Model Portfolio at davidjwaldron.com as of the period ending June 30, 2020.
Note: All figures are trailing multiples (times x for TTM.)

Table Key

- P/S — price to sales.
- P/E — price to earnings.
- P/CF — price to operating cash flow.
- EV/OE — enterprise value to operating earnings or earnings before interest, taxes, depreciation, and amortization.

At the time of these valuation multiple calculations, we were in the early innings of a coronavirus pandemic, a potential sustained bear market, or perhaps a stock price rebound following the COVID-19 correction of an inflated bull market. For example, I isolated the five holdings from the constituents in The Model Portfolio screened from about 2,500 US exchange-traded companies in the communication services, consumer discretionary, consumer staples, health care, industrials, and technology sectors.

The market was presuming that cord-cutting fears for Comcast remained in perpetuity. The CVS assimilation of health insurer Aetna was still on the radar. As the market was predicting for every retailer, Kroger was falling victim to Amazon's conquering of the space as the sole source of consumer goods, despite antitrust laws. The grounding of the Boeing 737 MAX jet model had blindsided Southwest Airlines—a premier capital allocator in the industry—and the travel industry was taking a further hit from COVID-19. Plus, the global new car sales slowdown was affecting Toyota. Nonetheless, each of the five equities was a prime example of a quality operator trading at an apparent value price.

Asleep at the Wheel

As of the June 30, 2020 update, engine maker Cummins (NYSE: CMI) was the only company on my watchlist that met or exceeded all five of The Model Portfolio's preferred methodologies. However, I missed buying it at a steep discount during the market correction in March of 2020. Since my wife Suzan was recovering from heart surgery at the time, I have forgiven myself for missing this bargain and remain confident that another buying opportunity for CMI will present itself sooner than later.

A reminder that value-based common stock investing is the equivalent of finding the proverbial needle in a haystack and, therefore, requires large doses of discipline and patience for long-term success. Wait for the valuation multiples of the shares of an enduring enterprise to drop to levels signaling a temporary bargain. Just as discounted prices on Nike athletic wear appear on rare occasions, so do fair prices on Nike common stock. Keep your eyes open to avoid blinking and missing those excellent yet fleeting buying opportunities.

Other Conventional Valuation Multiples

Three supplemental ratios are commonplace in valuing stock prices. In practice, I place less weight on these pricing models.

Price to Book Value

The price-to-book ratio (P/B) measures the stock price relative to stockholders' equity or net asset value on a trailing quarter basis. Focus on the stocks of companies with sound fundamentals selling at a P/B ratio of fewer than two times. Finding such an attractive trading multiple at a quality company is rare in a secular bull market. During those times, look for P/B values below the industry average.

Some investors prefer a measurement of the tangible book, where intangible items such as patents, intellectual property, and goodwill are absent from the denominator. Although accounting for intangible assets is more often an exercise in allowable balance sheet bloat, confirm management is limiting manipulation of the entries and is consistent from quarter to quarter.

Price to Forecasted Earnings

Despite my perpetual skepticism in forecasting and frustration from readers it sometimes elicits, the forward price-to-earnings ratio (P/FE) is worth a peek if you are looking to tip the balance on a well-researched stock. Remember, as a future indicator, placing a heavier weight on P/FE risks venturing into a speculative, roll-of-the-dice crapshoot. Use P/FE as a tiebreaker instead of a tie maker.

Price to Earnings Growth

The price-to-earnings-growth ratio (PEG) is the P/E ratio divided by the consensus longer-term EPS growth rate forecast provided by brokerage firm analysts based on guidance from senior executives. The PEG ratio emerged as a favorite among the growth and momentum crowds. The value investor remains cautious based on the forward projection formula of PEG as opposed to actual trailing results. Nevertheless, PEG provides a substantive peek into the price worthiness of a stock. Target a PEG ratio of fewer than two times in general, or at least below the industry average.

Buy Something When No One Likes It

> " *The safest and most potentially profitable thing is to buy* "
> *something when no one likes it.*[1]
>
> —HOWARD MARKS

This chapter closes with another simple yet profound quote from the client memos of Howard Marks compiled for his seminal book *The Most Important Thing*.

In the spirit of Marks' wisdom, I added each stock to The Model Portfolio based on initial bullish ratings in the valuation multiples. The other four areas of my proprietary research methodology: value proposition, shareholder yields, return on management, and up next in Chapter Fifteen: downside risk, weighed in as well. Regardless of the valuation multiples or methods a retail investor employs, remember that price is what you pay; value is what you get. It is worth repeating that value matters in every area of our financial lives, including the stock market, and endures through each market cycle for decades to come, and perhaps forever.

The lesson remains the same: Own slices of quality businesses, purchased when the stock price is deemed reasonable or trading at temporary bargain prices after being shunned by the crowd.

* * *

CHAPTER FOURTEEN SUMMARY

On Intrinsic Value

- A primary tenet in the search for alpha from investing in common stocks is determining the attractiveness of a stock price based on valuation multiples relative to the fundamentals of the company.

- An appealing stock price becomes a nonnegotiable prerequisite to initiating the productive partial ownership of a quality business.

■ In weighing valuation, focus on the price multiples of trailing sales, earnings, and operating cash flow, and the market sentiment meter of enterprise value relative to operating earnings.

■ Although helpful as valuation multiples, be wary of the intangibles of price-to-book ratios and the speculative projections of future growth and earnings.

■ Buy the common shares of a targeted, high-quality, enduring company when the market turns against it, thereby generating a bargain price point.

Fifteen

Assess Downside Risk

M anaging downside risk is more controllable than trying to predict future returns. A top priority of the defensive investor is the preservation of capital; thus, assessing downside risk is an essential research component and measurement tool of the thoughtful investor.

Seek profitable, dividend-paying, wide and narrow moat companies that are less volatile than the market on the whole and have the free cash flow and liquidity to pay the bills, both short- and long-term. Nonetheless, as an active investor, you want to be aware of the perils of investing in the common shares of publicly traded companies.

Any market downturn, regardless of the cause or ultimate duration, delivers a stark reminder that managing risk is paramount to the disciplined investor. This chapter covers how to screen company risk profiles toward uncovering quality stocks with the highest potential for a limited downside to protect your precious invested capital. In doing so, you assign a grade to an individual common stock based on several measures of investment risk.

Outperformance Happens on the Downside as Well

Although a trading day, week, month, or quarter never defines a market sample size, in my personal experience, market outperformance is achieved more often on the downside. A portfolio of quality companies purchased at sensible prices that underperforms the market when it is flying high has the propensity to outperform the market on the downswing, thus increasing the potential to exceed the market over time.

I rely on select broad indicators that measure the downside risk of the stocks held in our family portfolio or residing on The Model Portfolio watchlist. Any sudden downturn in the market reminds me of the cornerstone of disciplined investing: understanding the downside risk profile for each holding.

A practical exercise of the self-directed investor is due diligence in uncovering and managing the downside risk of owned or targeted publicly traded companies. Those assessing risk sufficiently may experience less volatility in bear market cycles or during corrections from surprise socioeconomic or geopolitical events.

Lessons in Risk Management

Markets are forever rising or capitulating. Trying to time the inevitable roller coaster ride is the stock market equivalent of predicting volcanic eruptions. Nevertheless, many investors embark on such a journey despite a subconscious understanding of the contrary.

The counterproductive way to managing investment risk is the equivalent of the herd riding the gravy train up the mountain with a self-assured buy and getting caught in a runaway train down to the valley resulting in a money-losing sell. Second-level investors do the exact opposite by becoming sellers as stocks trend upward and buyers as the market heads south. The pattern followed by the disciplined, value-based investor generates profits from the inept who act against glaring lessons from market history.

An investor or trader foreseeing the next market trend or target price with accuracy is as rare as a sports bettor who predicted the Philadelphia Eagles' defeat of the favored New England Patriots in Super Bowl LII. The win was destined after the Eagles executed a fourth-down trick pass play for the record books. The daring play at the end of the second quarter resulting in the first quarterback touchdown reception in the history of Super Sunday was indeed risky. If my memory serves me, in post-game interviews, Eagles head coach Doug Pederson implied it was a play the team practiced with diligence and brought to the game with the confidence to execute it with precision.

The lesson for the disciplined investor is that a risk assessed, understood, and well-managed is a risk worth taking.

Returns Are Unpredictable — Risk Is Controllable

Measuring, understanding, and accepting the downside price risk of a company and its common shares from an unforgiving market offer the best opportunities for investing with a tolerable, asymmetric risk/reward profile. Often, successful investors are rewarded more for limited portfolio downside in bear markets from a disciplined approach to risk-managed investing than from the upside in bull markets driven by exuberant participants.

The inevitable downturns develop into official corrections—defined as 10 percent off the market closing highs—or head fake buying opportunities in a continuing bull market, as happened often during the post-Great Recession boom. Regardless of the cause and effect, it is imperative to understand your risk profile in advance of buying common shares, including those of value-priced, quality companies.

When executing, the patient investor is enjoying the magic of annualized compounding of total return over several market cycles from an acute understanding of the downside risk from a cast net encompassing a wide margin of safety. The defensive investor revisits the risk profiles of the holdings with regularity following the initial purchase.

I focus on four vital areas of a business that assess the measurable risk of the underlying stock in the context of its potential behavior in a down market cycle. The goal is to buy the stock when the overall measure of the downside is below the perceived market tolerance for acceptable risk.

Economic Moat

Within investing parlance, an *economic moat* is the subjective measure of the competitive advantages of the goods or services of a company in the marketplace. A wider moat creates a perceived barrier to entry for potential competitors. An economic moat is the unique competitive advantage—wide, narrow, or none—an enterprise has over other companies within the same industry. The financial media widely credits Warren Buffett for coining the term.

Morningstar is the leading proprietary data provider of economic moat ratings. Consider owning stocks of companies that Morningstar assigns wide, or at least narrow, moats. In theory, these stocks tend to have higher floors in down markets owing to superior competitive advantages. If a Morningstar moat rating is unavailable for your targeted equity, conduct your due diligence, and assign a rating of wide, narrow, or none. Although a simple exercise, assigning your stock a moat rating requires some thought and a pinch of common sense.

Classic wide-moat companies in The Model Portfolio included Coca-Cola (KO) because of its ubiquitous brand name, Nike (NKE), led by the globally recognized Swoosh, and Microsoft (MSFT) for its legacy computing supremacy from the Windows franchise. Although Morningstar assigns Toyota Motor (TM) a moat rating of none, the automaker's legendary reputation for quality equates to at least a narrow competitive advantage and thus is an exception to the rule.

A company enjoying market dominance within a limited pool of competitors, or oligopoly, is an ideal wide-moat play for the value investor. Oligopolies are more attractive to investors than monopolies, as the single dominant player is vulnerable to government antitrust enforcement at home and abroad.

Debt Coverage

Debt can be the lifeblood of a growing business or its death knell. Dive into the last quarter's balance sheet and look for three telltale signs of the ability of management to limit debt to sufficient levels. Benjamin Graham wanted to know the companies he owned as a shareholder were capable of covering debt in the face of a crisis. Hence, he bought slices of companies with balance sheets exhibiting the capacity to pay down short- and long-term debt with liquid assets. Graham's rule offers timeless advice for investors.

Trading distressed debt is standard practice in the financial services industry; investing in a business without understanding the leverage and debt coverage is perhaps riskier than the obligation itself.

Long-Term Debt Coverage

An essential measure of the downside risk is the long-term debt coverage of a company. For example, the metric of current assets (CA) divided by long-term debt (LTD) represents the equivalent of balance sheet liquidity for a publicly traded company. The CA/LTD metric demonstrates the strategic capacity for management to pay down debt in a crisis.

Long-term debt coverage was a favorite of Graham's. Higher than one-and-a-half times is ideal, as you want to own businesses capable of paying down debt at least 150 percent above the current level using liquid assets. In simple terms, the company can pay off any long-term debt obligations using current assets such as cash and equivalents, short-term investments, accounts receivables, and inventories. In theory, companies with CA/LTD lower than one are unable to pay off 100 percent of debt obligations using liquid or current assets.

Long-term debt coverage is the leading downside risk indicator of The Model Portfolio.

Debt to Equity

Avoid leveraged companies carrying long-term debt more than double the outstanding equity. Just as leveraged households often carry debt loads that exceed net worth, the same holds for many companies. Using debt in a low-interest-rate environment is judicious; leveraging too far beyond net worth or net asset value creates a recipe for disaster — waiting for a market downturn or economic recession to cook the books. The economic impact of the COVID-19 pandemic was a stark reminder of the rampant illiquidity of households and businesses.

The good times are euphoric until they're not.

Short-Term Debt Coverage or Current Ratio

Measuring short-term debt coverage via the current ratio (CR) is another simple yet telling measure of the financial stability of a company. The current ratio is total current assets divided by total current liabilities for the same period; the higher above one, the better.

The current ratio measures the short-term debt coverage to demonstrate if the liquid assets of the targeted or owned business are adequate in funding short-term liabilities such as accounts payable, accrued expenses, debt service, and income taxes. Thus, CR measures the short-term balance sheet liquidity of the operation.

Although the above three ratios have served The Model Portfolio well, several other debt measures exist, including ones relative to free cash flow, capital, and interest coverage. Whatever your choices, beware of the burden of debt as it decimates even the most competitive of enterprises.

Stock Price Volatility or Beta

Beta is the fluctuation of a stock price to changes in the overall market and gauges the volatility of traded shares. Although a controversial metric, look at the five-year trailing beta to see how movements in the stock price measure up to market volatility or lack thereof. Nonetheless, remember that risk is more related to the permanent loss of capital than up-and-down price movements.

As its primary benchmark, the US stock market assigns the S&P 500 a perpetual beta of one. Despite the low market volatility of the post-Great Recession, I still contemplated beta in my research, targeting a trailing beta below one and a quarter or fewer than 25 percent volatility to the benchmark. A beta that is lower than one and a quarter is ideal insurance for protecting your invested capital. If you want to bypass companies with the makings for significant downsides, avoid stocks with high betas.

The holdings of The Model Portfolio—as of the June 30, 2020 close—had a cumulative average weighted beta of 0.92. The portfolio tends to outperform the market on significant down days, and such optimum behavior is perhaps a reflection of beta. Hence, own shares of companies with a history of outperformance in declining markets regardless of the level of performance in up markets. Remember, the best opportunity to outperform the market, in the long run, is to beat it on those down days, weeks, months, or entire bear markets.

Low-beta common stocks contribute to a positive down market portfolio strategy by limiting potential losses. Any upside market activity generates profits for your portfolio.

Short Interest

The short interest as a percentage of the float is the ratio of tradeable common shares sold short on a bet the stock price is poised to drop because of decaying fundamentals, high valuation multiples, or negative catalysts, among other special situations. It indicates the level of market sentiment by informing us if the herd is betting the price of a stock will fall. Short interest represents the percentage of outstanding shares investors have borrowed to sell short and have yet to cover or close out the positions.

A short trader's tongue-twister: Shorts in time are left short and cover their shorts before losing their shirts. Defer shorting of the market to the professionals who walk the tightrope of such speculative practices. Nevertheless, don't worry about the prospects of the market plundering a mid- or large-cap stock if the short interest is below 10 percent of the float.

Whether the bets are right or wrong, higher short interest on a stock signals that investors think something is awry with the fundamentals of the company, the valuation of the underlying shares, or the state of the subindustry encompassing the enterprise. Thus, it is in your best interest to avoid such stocks upfront or investigate if your current holding or targeted buy converts to a proving ground for short-sellers.

Buying stocks sold short at high levels is more akin to deep value trading than to exceptional value investing. The buy-and-hold investor—a.k.a. the long side—needs to be aware of any counterintelligence against the stock. Think of short interest as the hedge fund consensus since the Wall Street money manager elite executes a significant shorting of stocks.

Assigning a Downside Risk Profile

In this chapter, you learned to assess the competitive advantages of a business, including the width of its economic moat.

Next, you evaluated the long-term, short-term, and equity debt coverage or liquidity of the balance sheet. You then measured the volatility of the stock regarding the trailing beta and took a peek at the short interest or the so-called smart money's take on the prospects of the stock.

Now, assign an overall downside risk rating to your actual or watchlist holding. Determine the grade for a company and the common stock based on your weighted measures of investment risk. Designate an overall market risk profile of high, above-average, average, below-average, or low to each stock researched. Equities interpreted as buy-and-hold candidates often present with below-average or low downside risk profiles.

As an exception, purchase or hold average or above-average risk-rated stocks if your due diligence suggests the other areas of your quantitative and qualitative assessments outweigh the higher-risk profile. I have never initiated or stayed long with any stockholding rated as high-risk. Preserving capital on the downside always supersedes the pursuit of any potential upside.

Manage the Downside — Let the Upside Take Care of Itself

" To me, risk is the most interesting, challenging, and essential aspect of investing.[1]

—HOWARD MARKS

The inevitable reminder or repeated lesson of unexpected and sudden downturns in the stock market, an industry, or a company is limiting ownership to the stocks of enterprises that you have assessed the downside risk as manageable and tolerable. In the wisdom of Howard Marks opening this section, successful portfolio management lies in the ability of the investor to understand and manage the controllable downside risk as opposed to the impossible task of predicting market movements and stock prices.

The market releases the bulls or the bears at its convenience and, therefore, requires preparation on our part. Counter with established ownership of quality companies that perhaps run with bulls when the mood allows, but, of utmost importance, are less inclined to retreat with or go as far as the bears.

Although lowering the downside risk is preferable, zero liability is unobtainable, such as during a market downturn. I have learned from experience and observation that stocks rated with low and below-average risk grades have the propensity to decline less than the S&P 500 or the market on the whole during crashes or downturns.

Assessing downside risk is paramount to the ultimate success of the thoughtful, disciplined, and patient investor.

* * *

CHAPTER FIFTEEN SUMMARY

On Assessing Downside Risk

- Managing downside risk is more controllable than trying to predict future returns.

- High-quality common stocks offer the best opportunities for your portfolio to outperform the market on the downside, with a lesser percentage drop than benchmark index averages.

- A risk understood, accepted, and well-managed becomes a risk worth taking.

- To assess the downside risk of a targeted company, focus on the economic moat and debt coverage of the enterprise; and on the price volatility and short interest in the outstanding shares.

- The thoughtful, disciplined, and patient investor manages the downside risk and lets the upside take care of itself.

* * *

PART II: STRATEGIES

- ○ What other strategies have you discovered and rely on when selecting the common shares of quality businesses for your portfolio?

III

PRACTICES

Sixteen

Construct A Common Stock Portfolio

This chapter brings the book's principles and strategies together by building a template to screen common stocks for further research toward inclusion in a longer-view, self-managed portfolio with market-beating potential.

Use the template for checking the quality and value of your current common stock holdings or for targeted companies on—or to add to—your watchlist.

How to Use The Model Portfolio as a Proxy

I rate each stock holding in The Model Portfolio with a current view of bullish, neutral, or bearish.

- Bullish equates to buy or add.

- Neutral equates to hold or watch.

- Bearish equates to sell or reduce.

Please note the assigned stock ratings in The Model Portfolio are my opinion; you must conduct independent due diligence or seek professional advice before making investment decisions.

Although I am partial to the long-term prospects of every company in The Model Portfolio, I buy or add to the equities rated bullish in valuation multiples or those stocks I viewed as undervalued at the time of the analysis. Since each stock was rated bullish when added to the portfolio, keep an eye out for new additions, as I never add a position to the portfolio unless the initial view is bullish. As the portfolio matures, neutral ratings become commonplace; however, each holding has the potential to return to a bullish rating from unexpected market conditions or receive the dreaded bearish call following the deterioration of company fundamentals. Since I restrict the use of index ETFs to hedges, those holdings are unrated in The Model Portfolio.

In summary, I equal-weight The Model Portfolio for tracking benchmark performance. I also equal-weight our real-time family portfolio allocations, and on occasion, add quality companies with good, long-term prospects trading at fair prices and thereby rate as bullish in portfolio updates. I publish the current views at any time, quarterly at a minimum.

Common Stock Portfolio Research Template

Do-it-yourself or retail-level common stock investment research is best carried out within a model or outline driving to a qualitative and quantitative, unbiased conclusion of a bullish, neutral, or bearish call on the targeted company and the stock representing ownership.

The main drivers of the research template are to formulate a thesis of opinion by analyzing the publicly traded business and the underlying stock. Presented in Part II: Strategies, the research modalities include:

- The value proposition the enterprise presents to its customers, including the products or services offered and the competitive landscape.

- The average of the total shareholder yields to measure how the stock compares to the Ten-Year Treasury rate.

- The fundamentals of the company, including the strength of senior management.

- The valuation of the common shares or intrinsic value.

- The downside risks of the company and the stock.

The template may include an analysis of the market consensus to measure overall sentiment and employee satisfaction. Most important is analyzing the common stock to search for ample reasons why the business is worthy of a slice of ownership or the reasons you are choosing to pass. In essence, research the company and tell a story in your investment thesis. The disciplined investor performs bottom-up analysis focused on finding quality companies regardless of the specific industry or any macro conditions of the general economy forever guaranteed to be fickle.

You are free to use this template as a guide to determine if a targeted publicly traded company and the representative common shares are worthy of further research and due diligence for potential inclusion in your portfolio.

Large- and Mid-Cap Exchange-Traded Equities

Target the US major exchange-traded—NYSE and NASDAQ—common shares of high-quality, dividend-paying companies.

Avoid over-the-the-counter issues (OTC) and micro caps as speculative. Focus on mid-caps and large-caps, leaving the more speculative—albeit worthy—small-caps to the professional, lowest-cost fund managers. The mid- and large-cap common shares traded on the major exchanges provide a potentially wider margin of safety for longer-term investing.

You have achieved true alpha when your small-caps become mid-caps, and your mid-caps become large-caps. Although large-caps sometimes become mega-caps, each may also regress to mid-caps and small-caps, or worse, no caps.

Market cap reflects sentiment. Contributing an appealing stock price of a quality enterprise notwithstanding, pay less attention to the existing crowd-think as long as the stock is compounding over the long-term at a rate as good as, if not better than, expected at purchase. Pay more attention to the value proposition of the products or services of the operation plus the allocation of capital by management than any investor sentiment.

Objectives and Strategies of The Model Portfolio

To support the mission of finding value with wide margins of safety, then building wealth from the magic of compounding through every market cycle, my author website *davidjwaldron.com* offers its members a diverse model mirroring my real-time family portfolio. The holdings of the portfolio offer do-it-yourself, long-view value investors excellent ideas worthy of further due diligence.

I support The Model Portfolio with the corresponding user guide, daily performance tracker, quarterly spreadsheet, and supporting narrative report. The portfolio is exclusive to active members of my website; please remember to sign up at davidjwaldron.com. As of the writing of this edition of the book, the service is complimentary.

This section shares the profile, objectives, and strategies of The Model Portfolio to give you a framework for targeting the holdings that best fit your investment objectives.

Portfolio Profile

The Model Portfolio represents a non-marketable, illustrative composition of the publicly traded common shares of quality large- and mid-cap companies held in our family portfolio. Each has the potential for superior compounding of total return—capital gains plus income from dividends—protected by a margin of safety to deliver alpha across each market cycle.

The concentrated portfolio reflects the challenge of finding new ideas as worthy as any of the current holdings. Always the proverbial two-edged sword, an over-diversified basket of stocks is best served by reducing holdings or using passive index hedging to lessen risk and lower costs.

Concentrated portfolios of select quality compounders purchased at reasonable prices are the best opportunity for success in long-term, do-it-yourself common stock investing.

Portfolio Objectives

The Model Portfolio seeks long-term compounding growth of both principal and income. Achieving a satisfactory current income from regular dividends is paramount to the total-return objective; therefore, a company must pay a regular dividend for the common shares to be eligible for inclusion in the portfolio.

Portfolio Strategies

The Model Portfolio represents a concentrated basket of the liquid, publicly traded, common shares of the large- and mid-capitalization companies available on the major US exchanges.

In selecting components for The Model Portfolio, the focus is on the stocks of quality companies appearing undervalued by the market against a favorable long-term outlook for total-return compounding protected by acceptable levels of risk. I selected constituents for The Model Portfolio from the research and analysis of qualitative and quantitative measures of the company with a bias toward the strategies of value proposition, shareholder yields, return on management, valuation multiples, and downside risk.

Due diligence focuses on the products or services, free cash flow, return on invested capital, the stock price, and the debt coverage of the company. I approach portfolio construction from Warren Buffett's premise of *price is what you pay; value is what you get.*

I benchmark the performance of The Model Portfolio to the S&P 500 Index. To measure the overall long-term performance of each holding, the representative stocks of The Model Portfolio are equal-weighted against the benchmark.

Although The Model Portfolio positions are concentrated by design, for the sake of variety to benefit subscribers, what were perhaps good ideas at the time are removed and replaced with new, more promising common stocks, when appropriate. Keep in mind, when implementing changes to the portfolio, I often delay notification to members until the next quarterly update.

Stock Screen User Guide and Definitions

Next, let's pull together the principles and strategies discussed throughout the book by building a stock screen and portfolio tracker. The stock screen used to construct The Model Portfolio favors the protocols of finding stock price value from wide margins of safety, then profiting from price and dividend compounding driven by high returns on capital allocations.

The purpose of the screen is to cultivate a list of companies worthy of additional research for possible long-term ownership, as opposed to trading stocks on speculation in the hopes of fast money.

Holes in the Screen

Be cautious when using screens to research stocks, limiting any use to separating the wheat from the chaff. Because of the propensity to eliminate quality enterprises, never use screeners for outright investment decisions. You are the stock selector following further due diligence.

Each of these calculations is available at your online discount broker or other free financial sites on the internet, such as Google Finance and Yahoo Finance. I have found GuruFocus, Seeking Alpha, and Morningstar helpful for individual stock research as well; however, each of those sites does require paid subscription upgrades to access certain levels of information.

THE VALUE PROPOSITION

- **Sector** is the market classification of a group of related industries and includes communication services, consumer discretionary, consumer staples, energy, financials, real estate, health care, materials, industrials, technology, and utilities. Stick with sectors and industries within your circle of competence. Please note The Model Portfolio stock screen does not include sectors outside of my sphere of acquired expertise: energy, financials, real estate, materials, and utilities. Again, avoided are the speculative commodity-driven energy and materials sectors, although I am empathetic to retirees investing in financials, REITs, and utilities for stable income opportunities.

- **Major exchange** is whether shares are trading on either the New York Stock Exchange (NYSE) or NASDAQ, including American depositary receipts (ADRs) of foreign-based companies. No over-the-counter (OTC) issues because of the more speculative and illiquid trading paradigm.

- **Market capitalization** denotes whether the market has capitalized the stock as a large- or mid-cap company. Avoid small- and micro caps as too volatile and speculative. No penny stocks or any issues that are trading at less than five to ten dollars a share.

- **Products and services** are the offerings of the company, whether tangible goods or intangible services. Avoid taking ownership slices of businesses with sophisticated or confusing products and services. In the wisdom of Peter Lynch, "Buy what you know and understand."[1]

- **Closing share price** is the market price of one share of common stock as of the last reported quarter-end closing date.

- **Prior quarter adjusted close** is the market price of one share of stock as of the previous quarter-end date.

- **Quarter-to-date total-return** (QTD) is the increase (or decrease) percentage of the closing share price from the previous quarter, adjusted for dividends and stock splits.

- **One-year average total return** is the gain/loss in stock price, adjusted for dividends and splits since the last market close for the twelve months preceding the previous period end date.

- **S&P 500 one-year total return** is the gain/loss of the benchmark index price—adjusted for dividends and splits—since the last market close for the twelve months preceding the previous period end date.

- **Value proposition rating** is bullish, neutral, or bearish based on your definition of the overall value proposition of the company, condensed into an elevator pitch.

SHAREHOLDER YIELDS

- **Earnings yield** (EY) is the inverse of the price-to-earnings ratio (P/E). Earnings yield indicates how much a company earns each year per common share relative to the share price. The earnings per share or EPS represent the portion of the profits of the operation allocated to each outstanding share of common stock. Target an EY of more than 6 percent or the equivalent of a P/E multiple of below seventeen times.

- **Free cash flow yield** (FCFY) indicates how much a company generates in free cash flow each year per common share relative to the share price. Free cash flow per share is free cash flow divided by shares outstanding as of the end of the most recent fiscal period. Target an FCFY of 7 percent and higher or the equivalent of fewer than fifteen times the inverted price-to-free cash flow multiple.

- **Dividend yield** (one-year average) indicates how much a company paid out in averaged dividends for the trailing twelve months relative to the share price. Limit trailing twelve-month rates to below 5 or 6 percent to avoid high-yield equity junk.

- **Average of total yields** averages earnings, free cash flow, and dividend yields per share.

- **Ten-Year Treasury rate** is the prevailing yield on the Ten-Year Treasury benchmark note.

- **Shareholder rating** is bullish, neutral, or bearish based on the company average of total yields as compared to the Ten-Year Treasury rate.

RETURN ON MANAGEMENT

- **Revenue growth** is the compounded annual three-year growth rate of company revenues or net sales. Avoid negative revenue growth.

- **Net profit margin** is the percent of revenues remaining after paying operating expenses, interest, and taxes divided by sales for the trailing twelve months. Seek profitable companies to avoid speculation.

- **Return on equity** (ROE) is the income available to common shareholders for the trailing twelve months divided by the average ownership equity of the common stockholders from the most recent fiscal period and the year-earlier fiscal period, expressed as a percentage. Reveals how much profit a company generates from shareholder investment in the stock. Consider targeting an ROE of 15 percent and higher.

- **Return on invested capital** (ROIC) is net income after taxes divided by the average of total equity plus the sum of total long-term debt, total other liabilities, deferred income tax, and minority interest, expressed as a percentage. Measures how well a company is using its working capital to generate returns. Target an ROIC above 12 percent.

- **Weighted average cost of capital** (WACC) calculates the cost of capital of the corporation, weighing each category in proportion. The ROIC needs to exceed the WACC by a comfortable margin, giving credence to the ability of management to outperform the capital costs.

- **Management rating** is bullish, neutral, or bearish based on your weighting of the overall return on management.

VALUATION MULTIPLES

- **Price-to-sales** (P/S) ratio is the closing price divided by the sum of sales per share over the trailing twelve months. Price-to-sales measures stock price relative to revenue. Target a P/S of fewer than two times.

- **Price-to-trailing earnings** (P/E) is the closing price divided by the sum of GAAP diluted earnings per share (EPS) over the trailing twelve months. Although an arbitrary multiple, target a P/E of fewer than 17 times or below the benchmark industry averages.

- **Price-to-operating cash flow** (P/CF) is the previous closing stock price divided by cash flow per share for the most recent fiscal year. For the best value, target single-digit multiples.

- **Enterprise value to operating earnings** (EV/EBITDA) is the market capitalization plus debt, minority interest, and preferred shares, minus total cash and cash equivalents (EV), divided by earnings before interest, taxes, depreciation, and amortization (EBITDA). Measures whether a stock is overbought—a bearish or neutral signal, or oversold—a bullish or neutral signal by the market. Target an EV/EBITDA of fewer than 12 times.

- **Valuation rating** is bullish, neutral, or bearish based on your weighting of the valuation multiples of the common stock or portfolio on the whole.

DOWNSIDE RISK

- **Economic moat** is the competitive advantage—wide, narrow, or none—that a company has over other businesses within the same industry. Target companies that own wide or narrow moats.

- **Long-term debt coverage** measures current assets (CA) divided by long-term debt (LTD). Demonstrates balance sheet liquidity or a company's capacity to pay down debt in a crisis, if necessary. Generally, one-and-a-half times long-term debt to current assets is ideal.

- **Current liabilities coverage** or the current ratio (CR) is the total current assets divided by total current liabilities for the same period. CR measures the short-term liquidity of the balance sheet. Target higher than one time, although a quality company sometimes has a CR of less than one because of the industry served.

- **Beta** gauges the volatility or systemic risk of a stock in comparison to the market as a whole. Use a five-year beta trend line and screen for companies with betas lower than one and a quarter. The S&P 500 beta is constant at one.

- **Short interest** represents the percentage of outstanding shares that investors have borrowed to sell short and have yet to cover or close the position. The short interest provides a sentiment indicator that the market is betting the price of a stock will fall. Be wary of shares if the short interest exceeds 10 percent of the float, an indicator of a possible speculative deep value play.

- **Downside risk rating** is the grade, such as low, below-average, average, above-average, or high, you assign to a stock based on the weighted measures of investment risk.

PORTFOLIO PERFORMANCE

- **Added to the portfolio** is the date you initiated a position in the common stock.

- **Entry price per share** is the price you paid for each share of common stock adjusted for splits and dividends. Note: If you are a value-based investor, consider having dividends paid to cash.

- **Total return since added** is the equal-weighted, average total return for the stock or the portfolio as a whole since the date added to your portfolio, adjusted for splits and dividends.

- **S&P 500 on purchase date** reflects the closing price, adjusted for dividends, of the S&P 500 (.INX) on the date of the corresponding stock purchase.

- **S&P 500 relative performance** is the equal-weighted, to-date performance of the S&P 500 Index relative to the corresponding common stock or the portfolio on the whole.

- **Portfolio versus benchmark** is the equal-weighted return performance of the portfolio and its common stock components versus the benchmark S&P 500 Index for the same time frames.

SENTIMENT

- **Current view** of bullish, neutral, or bearish reflects the latest published call for each stock and the overall portfolio based on a review of each portfolio indicator, weighted toward the key attributes defining your valuation and margin of safety. The current view of The Model Portfolio provides a screenshot of the research as opposed to a definitive buy, hold, or sell signal.

Making the Portfolio Cut

Any stock surviving the screen becomes a candidate for additional research and potential real-time purchase or active inclusion in your portfolio. Highlighted in the next chapter, managing portfolio allocation—assigning capital and reinvested dividends to each common stock holding—is as important as asset allocation.

In Part I: Chapter Three, the margin of safety is presented as a principle of value investing where an investor purchases securities when the market price is well below the perceived intrinsic value. Although Wall Street uses standard formulas based on models projecting future free cash flows and other assumptions, the thoughtful investor on Main Street is forever wary of the assumptive projections of those formulas.

Base your margin of safety calculation on the valuation theory of finding mispriced stocks with good earnings and free cash flow yields, plus superior returns on invested capital exceeding the weighted average cost of the capital.

Favor liquid, long- and short-term debt coverage, countered by a perceived out-of-favor market sentiment as suggested by lower ratios of enterprise value to operating earnings, price-to-sales, and price-to-operating-cash flow.

Next, weigh the above key indicators to determine the overall equity bond rate, earnings quality, management effectiveness, financial stability, and market valuation of the targeted company. Seek longer-term investment in the stakeholders and products or services of quality, publicly traded companies as opposed to the shorter-term momentum trading or trend following of digitized, faceless stocks with limited utility.

Build a Portfolio with Market-Beating Potential

For the retail-level, long-view, value-based investor, the stock selection template of The Model Portfolio offers exceptional parameters to screen for ideas worthy of further due diligence. Since the present or future holdings are suggested ideas as opposed to recommendations, please conduct your research and read the accompanying disclosures in the Introduction before making any investments.

Regardless of diversification, investing in common stocks carries the risk of loss of invested capital attributable to company failures, irrational market sentiment, negative financial news, analyst downgrades, or surprise events. The US major exchange-traded large- and mid-caps tend to be less vulnerable to stock volatility and reduced market liquidity than the small and micro caps as well as over-the-counter issues.

Value traps or so-called falling knives are an unavoidable downside of stock-picking. The challenge is applying thought, discipline, and patience, plus a pinch of common sense in finding more good ideas in the present than good ideas at the time. Assuming equal allocation, if three or four out of five ideas are profitable, the losses from the one or two inferior ideas are offset or at least covered by the winners.

* * *

CHAPTER SIXTEEN SUMMARY

On Constructing a Retail Common Stock Portfolio

- Use The Model Portfolio template to construct a portfolio or to check the quality and value of your common stock holdings and targeted companies already on (or to add to) your watchlist. The Model Portfolio template is an illustrative research tool; you take responsibility for any ultimate investment decisions if choosing to use it.

- Create a portfolio profile by defining the mission, objectives, and strategies to give you a framework for targeting potential holdings that best fit your investment objectives.

- In the quest to keep investing super simple, the research modalities of the template are limited to the value proposition presented by the enterprise to its customers, the shareholder yields on the common stock, the strength of senior management, the valuation multiples of the common shares, plus the downside risk of the company and the underlying stock.

- Any stock surviving the screen becomes a candidate for additional research and potential real-time purchase or active inclusion in your portfolio. Always perform your due diligence and seek professional advice as warranted.

- Regardless of diversification, investing in common stocks carries the risk of losing invested capital owing to business failures, irrational market sentiment, negative financial news, analyst down-grades, and surprise events. Always invest with a margin of safety.

Seventeen

Manage Portfolio Allocation

Now that you have researched and perhaps purchased common shares of select companies, it is critical to begin managing your portfolio allocation strategies. Portfolio allocation, or how you assign securities, dividend payouts, and investable cash within your basket, is as important as the asset allocation of stocks, bonds, real estate, and money markets.

Members have queried me for universal suggestions on how to allocate investment capital when starting or maintaining a portfolio of common stocks hedged by indexed exchange-traded funds (ETFs). How does the independent investor initiate new investments or add holdings to a portfolio according to a weighting mechanism?

How do you reinvest dividends or store the cash as your dry powder in FDIC-insured money markets or sweep funds?

This chapter shares two standard options for portfolio allocation and why one method makes sense for the retail-level, buy-and-hold investor.

Weighting Mechanisms for Capital Allocation

The two universal portfolio weighting mechanisms are market-weight and equal-weight.

Introduced in Part I: Chapter Four was how the controversial use of market-cap-weighting dominates portfolio weighing mechanisms. Market cap, or capitalization-weighted indexes, assign component value by the total market value of the outstanding shares against the cumulative market cap of the investment basket. Thus, the largest market cap stock in the portfolio has the most significant influence on overall performance. Market capitalization is defined as the closing share price times the number of common shares outstanding.

By equal-weighting a portfolio, an investor treats each component the same regardless of price, market cap, or investor sentiment. As presented in Part I: Chapter Eight, there are other weighting mechanisms, such as free-float market-cap-weighted, price-weighted, and fundamental weighted.

The S&P 500 Index, the benchmark for The Model Portfolio, is free-float market-capitalization-weighted. With this method, a factor is assigned to each stock to account for the proportion of outstanding shares owned by the general public, as opposed to shares held by the government or company insiders.

The Dow Jones Industrial Average uses price weighting, where the higher-priced components receive the maximum weight. Fundamental weighting favors metrics such as sales, book value, dividends, cash flow, and earnings.

Choosing a Portfolio Allocation Option

Keep in mind that investing using a market-cap-weighted allocation translates to following the crowd, as the higher the market cap, the more popular the stock. I equal-weight our family portfolio and its public version, The Model Portfolio; the best approach to measuring overall performance against its benchmark.

To equal weight your portfolio, buy the same amount of dollars per holding or perhaps counter-weight using the same number of shares in different dollar amounts. Despite being partial to the stocks bought, you never know what holdings will outperform the benchmark in the long term. To maintain equal weighting in your portfolio, remember to rebalance at least once each year by reducing the winners and adding to underperformers meeting your valuation criteria. Equal-weighting has worked well for The Model Portfolio toward its market outperformance.

Attempting to bet what specific stocks or ETFs in your portfolio beat the market over an extended holding period is akin to trying to predict what teams win the Super Bowl, World Series, or March Madness in 2025 or 2030. Placing a speculative wager is perhaps the best we can muster. Making bets and crossing fingers is the antithesis of the thoughtful, disciplined, and patient investor. Equal-weight works best for buying and holding the mispriced, dividend-paying common shares of quality companies with compelling value propositions.

If we purchase bargain-priced stocks of well-managed, shareholder- and customer-friendly companies with excellent competitive advantages and palatable downside risk, the prospect exists that a majority of the holdings outperform the benchmark over time, such as the legacy holdings of The Model Portfolio. And the likelihood increases for the winners outnumbering the losers in the portfolio. Also, by equal-weighting, there is no need to overweight by speculating on what holdings will outperform the targeted benchmark.

Here are the total return performances—adjusted for stock splits and dividends—of the five original holdings of The Model Portfolio as of the quarter-end close on June 30, 2020.

Company	Walt Disney	3M	Union Pacific	Coca-Cola	Microsoft
Symbol	DIS	MMM	UNP	KO	MSFT
Added	6/15/09	7/21/10	8/9/10	10/4/10	6/28/11
Cost Basis	$20.88	$63.15	$29.26	$20.71	$20.87
Price	$111.51	$155.99	$169.07	$44.68	$203.51
Return	434.05%	147.02%	477.82%	115.74%	875.13%
S&P 500	198.42%	189.86%	174.90%	172.67%	139.10%

Performances of Original Five Holdings of The Model Portfolio
Source: The Model Portfolio at davidjwaldron.com. Period ending June 30, 2020.

Table Key

- ° Added — date added to The Model Portfolio.
- ° Cost Basis — cost per share adjusted for stock splits and dividends.
- ° Price — closing market price of the stock on June 30, 2020.
- ° Return — total return of stock since date added, as of June 30, 2020.
- ° S&P 500 — total return of benchmark index during the same timeline as holding period of corresponding stock as of June 30, 2020.

In the above sampling of five initial purchases for our family portfolio, three stocks have performed better than expected: DIS, UNP, and MSFT, and two have done worse than expected: MMM and KO. Investors are often surprised by the holdings outperforming and underperforming in a portfolio during an extended holding period. We never know until we do, although, after the fact, everything appears with 20/20 vision. Of course, the defensive Coke holding underperformed in a bull market.

How Value Investors Allocate Dividends

The automatic reinvestment of dividends is convenient if never the best approach to allocation.

Every investor has a preference when it comes to reinvesting dividends, whether choosing automatic reinvestment at your broker or using a company-sponsored dividend reinvestment plan (DRIP). Some investors also prefer dollar-cost averaging (DCA) or buying fixed dollar amounts of individual securities on a regular timetable. Each method has its benefits.

The hands-free automatic reinvestment plans are appealing and perhaps the best course for the passive investor. A traditional advantage of automatic reinvestment at your broker or using a DRIP program direct from the company was paying zero commissions on the trades. On the contrary, using dividend cash payments as dry powder entailed potential commissions on future trades. Nonetheless, the involuntary approach is often more expensive than the direct reinvestment of dry powder.

The disciplined, value-based investor, regardless of working on Wall Street or living on Main Street, is often leery of automatic reinvestment programs. Buying securities at your preferred price points, and ignoring the whims of the market, is the superior alternative. Allow dividends and capital gains distributions to settle as cash and reinvest the precious dry powder into the equities of quality companies when the prices are attractive.

Buy shares at low prices based on your perception of intrinsic value as opposed to the market's offering of the stock price at the moment of the automatic DCA or DRIP purchase. Although the recent trend of online brokers becoming commission-free is good news, continue to build up enough cash, accepting any commission or fees as an insignificant percentage of the gross amount on the trade. Either way, there is no excuse to overpay when reinvesting in the common shares of a company held in your portfolio.

Instead, follow the approach from the value investor playbook of buying equities on your terms as opposed to allowing the market to determine, for better or worse, your entry price. Have your online broker deposit dividend payments to an insured cash account. Tap into this accumulation of protected dry powder to purchase new or add to existing investments at bargain prices based on the valuation analysis discussed in Chapter Fourteen.

In the end, the choice lies with the investor based on comfort zones, as DRIP and DCA programs also provide a disciplined—albeit rigid—approach to personal investing. Dividends are often taken as cash by retirees as a means to provide supplemental income.

Understanding Your Opportunity Cost

As protection against an unexpected job loss, illness, or disability, it is essential to maintain built-in financial protections. The disciplined individual investor never allocates personal capital into stocks—or any investments with the risk of a total loss of the capital—needed to support the equivalent of a minimum of three to six months of nondiscretionary household expenses to finance the necessities of life. The thoughtful investor has a keen understanding of the opportunity cost of invested capital in the portfolio.

For example, any capital allocation to common stocks happens after determining the basics of life are accounted for, and the investment capital is underused in a well-funded money market or other low-earning financial instruments.

The ordinary expenses of life, including adequate future emergency funding, are covered before common stocks or other higher-risk investments are sought. And the thoughtful investor self-discloses with faith and honesty to loved ones that any capital allocated to an investment portfolio is indeed discretionary dollars.

If given a do-over as far as dollar contributions, I would dedicate 10 to 20 percent of my income to the stock market each year, going back to the summer jobs of my youth, never missing a beat from that point forward. Deducting 10 percent off the top of your income to invest in a retirement account and limiting your day-to-day budget with the remaining 90 percent is wise, solid financial planning. Greater than 10 percent is better if you classify the excess as discretionary dollars. Although rare for the common shares of quality companies to capitulate beyond the occasional temporary correction from a surprise event or bear market, execute responsible, prudent, and conservative capital allocations of your investment capital.

Sleep well tonight—and ten years from now—by understanding your opportunity costs.

Portfolio Performance is Paramount

In selecting the stocks researched, bought, or sold for my real-time family portfolio as reflected in The Model Portfolio, I aim to measure performance as a means of competing with myself—never with others—as a more productive way of living per motivational theory.*

By benchmarking The Model Portfolio and each of the individual holdings against the S&P 500, I measure performance from the date of acquisition or published research, adjusted for splits and dividends. Discovered over several market cycles and despite the laggards, it takes just a few big winners for a portfolio to beat the market over time. Once again, successful value investing requires a modest dose of common sense.

Build a collection of the dividend-paying common shares of quality companies purchased at sensible prices primed to outperform the benchmark across market cycles, or at least exceed any other expectations we have placed on us, as patient and disciplined investors. Despite the critical importance of each of the principles and strategies presented throughout this book, the essential dynamic is the preservation of invested capital.

Unlike trading, when practicing buy-and-hold, value-based common stock investing, selling is more the challenge than buying. Selling or reducing does make sense when raising capital to finance significant milestones in life or to expedite the occasional divestiture of an underperforming holding that was a good idea at the time of purchase.

* * *

*If intrigued, motivational principles and strategies are addressed more in-depth in two of my self-improvement books: *Hire Train Monitor Motivate* and *The Ten Domains of Effective Goal Setting*. The books are available for preview at your favorite online bookstore in your choice of paperback or ebook.

Self-managing an investment portfolio requires nothing more than thought, discipline, and patience. Consider equal-weighting your allocation to bypass the speculative trap of trying to predict what holdings will perform best long term. Forever practice responsible portfolio management with well-planned and executed allocations of available resources.

CHAPTER SEVENTEEN SUMMARY

On Portfolio Allocation

- Portfolio allocation, or how you assign investable capital and reinvested dividends to common stocks or ETF holdings, is as important as asset allocation.

- By equal-weighting a portfolio, the thoughtful investor treats each component the same regardless of price, market cap, or sentiment. The equal-weight approach negates the need to speculate by trying to predict which companies will outperform in the long run.

- The retail-level investor is often surprised by the holdings outperforming and underperforming in a portfolio over an extended period. Since hindsight is 20/20, you never know until you do.

- The patient and disciplined value investor allows dividends and capital gains distributions to settle as cash and reinvests those funds when prices are attractive.

- It takes just a few big winners for an entire portfolio to beat the market over time.

Eighteen

Control Portfolio Costs

This book advocates that, as a contrarian of the Wall Street way, the mantra of the common stock investor of Main Street is the relentless pursuit of the absolute return of capital and dividends with nominal fees and trading commissions. If using an investment advisor or subscribing to an investment service, remember to ask what is producing the better run rate for the advisor or author: the advisory and subscription fees or the returns on the investment picks?

I am proud our real-time family portfolio shared with the public as The Model Portfolio had produced far better returns from capital gains and dividends than the royalties from my published articles and former paid subscription service.

This chapter offers a primer on managing your portfolio—including cost controls—as if it were a small, home-based business.

Keep Your Portfolio Costs as Low as Possible

Never pay more than 1 percent of invested assets annualized in discount brokerage trading and fund advisory fees combined. It is unnecessary to pay more. The thoughtful investor incurs less than one-half of 1 percent in annualized fees and commissions on investments. Consider other, often-overlooked costs, such as 401(k) or 403(b), Traditional or Roth IRA, and 529 tuition plan fees, inflation, income taxes on dividends and capital gains, and subscription fees used to research and trade those investments. Thus, keeping direct portfolio fees annualized closer to 0.25 percent is paramount to an overall low-cost portfolio.

Furthermore, the disciplined retail investor refuses to allocate hard-earned dollars to any speculative, often high-cost investment such as commodities, high-yield or distressed debt, currencies, or abstract derivatives enjoyed by the Type-A personality Wall Street traders and speculators. Also avoid complicated, risky investment vehicles such as options, futures, or short-selling. Perhaps we are entertained by observing such exhilarating and speculative activity, albeit from the sidelines.

The bottom line to minimizing portfolio expenses involves picking cost-efficient investment vehicles such as dividend-paying common stocks and low-cost exchange-traded index funds, plus FDIC-insured cash instruments to store dry powder from contributions, capital gains, and dividends. Be cautioned that some funds and brokers are charging inexcusable fees for money markets and sweep funds as well. The Hamptons beach house churn comes from almost every investment category. Buy-and-hold is dead by convenience in the minds of those making a living on trading commissions and investment fees.

By controlling portfolio costs, you increase the potential for your family's portfolio to outperform the market benchmark over time. As individual situations vary, create a spreadsheet or table to plug in your investments and expenses to determine your overall cost of investing and the real bottom-line net gain of your portfolio. Just as with any business, be diligent in keeping your investment costs as low as possible to magnify contributions to your bottom line.

How to Keep Annualized Fees Below 1 Percent

Keeping fees and commissions well below 1 percent is paramount to a cost-efficient, self-managed investment portfolio. Although fees and commissions are the Wall Street way to the proverbial beach house in the Hamptons, what about market-beating real returns on capital invested?

Portfolio performance is an added benefit of the output of the financial elite when it occurs. The individual investor on Main Street must be wary of a myriad of other portfolio expenses eating away at total return. Regardless of investor level and whether institutional or retail, investing full-time, part-time, or in your spare time, focus on keeping your portfolio costs as low as possible. Being a defensive investor, I developed a model to measure the real costs of self-managing and sustaining a profitable investment portfolio.

I use an online discount broker when buying or selling common stocks or hedging with index ETFs. My broker now charges zero commissions per trade, and I limit any stakes in ETF or mutual fund hedges to those carrying fees below 0.50 percent per year. And yes, excellent, actively managed ETFs or mutual funds that charge below the typical annual advisory fees are available. Index funds are the best opportunity to stay below 0.25 percent. Nevertheless, be cautious of the low- or no-cost online discount brokers luring you into trading on margin and away from buy-and-hold investing.

The following table demonstrates a sample allocation of $5,000 invested in equal parts to four stocks from The Model Portfolio and an index ETF hedge annualized for three years to demonstrate controllable fee management. As presented in Part I: Chapter Eight, a hedge is an alternative investment used to offset the risk of common stock holdings, and this book advocates portfolio hedges limited to long-only index ETFs.

* * *

Company/Fund	Symbol	Initial$	Fees
Common Stocks			
Walt Disney	DIS	$1,000	$0.20
Coca-Cola	KO	$1,000	$0.20
Union Pacific	UNP	$1,000	$0.20
Microsoft	MSFT	$1,000	$0.20
ETF Hedge			
Vanguard S&P 500 ETF	VOO	$1,000	$9.20
Total	**Five**	**$5,000**	**$10.00**

Cost Analysis of Sample Stock Portfolio with ETF Hedge
Source: The Model Portfolio at davidjwaldron.com. Used for
illustration.

In the preceding table, the investor pays almost zero dollars a year in commissions and fees on the stocks and ETF, rounded up to include the ubiquitous penny service charges and slippage thrown into trades, and divided by three years.

Added next are the management fees for the ETF to calculate the total annualized percentage. At the time of this calculation, The Vanguard S&P 500 Index had an annual fee of just 0.03 percent or $3 per year on an average $1,000 balance.

The annualized cost of the sample portfolio over three years is less than 0.01 percent per year or about $3.33 in annual fees and commissions divided by $5,000 of initial capital. For a simple illustration, the example assumes no equity or income appreciation in the assets over the three years, countering the real-world desired result. Account value depreciation is also absent, although possible, such as during the COVID-19 coronavirus market correction.

A boon for the disciplined retail-level investor is the move to commission-free online trades allowing the occasional buys or sells at little or no cost. In the low-interest-rate, no-commission environment, the game for retail brokers now encompasses the leveraging of assets under management, order flow to market makers, and lending to accounts trading on margin.

Only Traders Worry About Spreads and Slippage

You may be thinking about the pitfalls of bid/ask spreads, such as hedging the price slippage from high-frequency trading with a limit order. I steer clear of trader mentality and leave it to the whim of the individual investor on how to purchase or sell securities in the least expensive, lowest-risk way. By using a reputable online discount broker, these issues are minimal in the scheme of things.

Billion-dollar institutional portfolios are affected by millisecond fluctuations in bid/ask spreads, prompting the professional portfolio manager to practice arbitrage and order limits to reduce price erosion from trading. In contrast, for the individual investor, mere pennies are lost on a smaller portfolio. Rest assured, the high-quality Main Street portfolio suffers insignificant, often undetected damage from price fluctuations at the time of the trade. Nonetheless, the annual percentage cost is relative.

Despite not accounting for capital gains or dividends, the preceding sample portfolio owns five quality positions for an annualized fee of less than one dollar per $1,000 invested, far lower than a 0.25 percent portfolio fee per year.

Be warned there are other, often-overlooked fees increasing portfolio costs.

Four Overlooked Threats to Cost-Efficiency

Although garnering widespread coverage from the financial media, the cost of investing goes far beyond just advisory management fees and broker commissions. The disciplined individual investor gauges several other significant threats to a portfolio's total return.

Here are four often-overlooked perils to the cost-efficiency of your portfolio, each involving more than just pursuing reduced fees or commissions.

401(k) Fees

Retirement consulting firms marketing 401(k) plans or similar non-profit and pension plans take, on average, about 0.50 percent of your balance just for administering the program. The skim is net of the management fees deducted from the mutual funds or ETFs within the menu of the investment choices offered by the plan. As a consequence, it is more challenging for the investor to keep the fund advisory fees below 1 percent in a company plan than in a self-managed account because of the incremental costs of the consulting firm.

The inherent benefits of employer-sponsored retirement plans such as tax deferments and contribution matches take precedent. Nevertheless, the cautionary tale of the cost/benefit asymmetry of a 401(k) or 403(b) plan is limiting your investment choices to the highest quality, lowest-cost funds.

Inflation

A significant threat of erosion in your investment portfolio is inflation.

The average annual rate of inflation in the United States between 1913 and 2018 was 3.15 percent.[1] Inflation fluctuates higher and lower year over year; thus, for the sake of argument, use an average of 3 percent per year as your benchmark.

The Rule of 72 in reverse dictates that with a 3 percent rate of inflation, the average cost of goods and services will be twice as high in 24 years as it is today. Your money is still there—if you haven't touched it—although it is buying half as much. Cash is never king when it comes to the imminent threat of inflation.

Income Taxes

As of this writing, the US federal government was taxing realized capital gains at 15 percent and dividends paid as ordinary income. According to the Tax Policy Center, in 2018, American taxpayers were subject to effective tax rates—including payroll taxes such as Social Security and Medicare—of between 2.9 percent on the lowest income spectrum and 29.6 percent on the highest income level.[2] Since the median effective tax rate was about 15.0 percent, I use that figure for illustration.

Subscriptions

Your financial newspapers or magazines, an investment newsletter, or online subscriptions also add costs to your portfolio. My expense model assumes $180 per year in typical overall subscription fees for the cost-conscious individual investor.

As far as any potential tax deductions, an individual investor must prorate costs tied to investing activity, and those costs may be tax-deductible. The same applies to fees and commissions. You are encouraged to consult a tax advisor for details on individual situations. Nonetheless, tax-deductible items are a cost to the portfolio.

Modeling the Real Cost of a Retail Portfolio

Using the above cost drivers in a typical self-managed portfolio, let's break down the real costs of the value-based retail investor. The estimated median savings for American families is about $60,000; thus, the model uses the figure for the total portfolio balance to measure overall costs to the investor. Based on examples and national averages covered in this chapter, the model assumes several parameters when calculating total portfolio costs.

- In the combined portfolio of $60,000, half is in a self-directed IRA or brokerage account, and half is in a 401(k) or similar employer-sponsored plan.

- Brokerage and IRA commissions are zero using an online discount broker with no account minimums.

- Combined 401(k) or equivalent employer-sponsored account fees are 1.00 percent annualized based on 0.50 percent administrator fees and 0.50 percent fund fees.

- The average annual inflation is 3 percent.

- The combined current and deferred effective tax rates of 15 percent, after deductions, assuming an average annual total return of 8 percent from dividends and capital gains or 1.20 percent of the portfolio balance.

- Conservative estimate of $180 per year in subscription costs.

* * *

Fee Category	Impact on Portfolio	$ Cost	% Cost
IRA/Brokerage Fees	$30,000 balance	$0	0.00%
401(k)/403(b) Fees	$30,000 balance	$300	0.50%
Inflation	$60,000 balance	$1,800	3.00%
Tax Liability	Dividends/capital gains	$720	1.20%
Subscriptions	Websites/newsletters	$180	0.30%
Total Portfolio Cost	**$60,000 balance**	**($3,000)**	**(5.00%)**
Portfolio Net Gain	**$60,000 balance**	**$1,800**	**3.00%**

Estimated Annual Costs of a Sample Self-Managed Portfolio
Source: davidjwaldron.com. Used for illustration. Note: % Cost represents aggregate of $60,000 portfolio. Tax liability represents current realized and deferred dividends and capital gains, but not deferred pre-tax income liability from retirement distributions.

Perhaps you consider an 8 percent average total return either as generous or conservative. Taking into account the historical total return for the S&P 500 is about 10 percent annualized, and assuming the lower-earning cash and fixed-income hedges represent about 25 percent of the total portfolio, you are looking at a minimum of an 8 percent average total return over a long-term horizon. Thus, the retail investor is sacrificing a mere two percentage points of the gain for the short-term safety of hedging with cash and bond holdings. Part I: Chapter Eight explores the concept of portfolio hedging.

A review of semantics justifies the sample portfolio balance is higher if you figure a positive historical annual total return, suggesting the numbers need adjusting. The model is for illustration, and in the context of several liabilities affecting a portfolio, the real cost erodes as much as two-thirds of the annual average gain. In this example, the basket experiences a 5 percent cost erosion of the presumed 8 percent gain.

The above example offers the sobering reality that a well-managed, cost-efficient, self-managed portfolio is getting a meager 3 percent net total return on the investments, based on an 8 percent average annual total return on capital and dividends. An even more somber thought is if you add a 1 percent professional money manager to the entire mix, the sample portfolio is netting a 2 percent average gain per year after subtracting the direct and indirect costs.

By realizing about 2 to 3 percent in net average annual gains after expenses and inflation; however, the individual investor is running a profitable portfolio. And that is why we invest: to beat nothing or the guaranteed return if you neglect to fund any portion of your earnings, or worse, three percent below nothing based on the historical inflation rate.

Limit Portfolio Turnover

Warren Buffett warns that if you are unwilling to hold a stock for ten years, you have no business in owning it for 10 minutes.[3] Another solution to keeping investment expenses low is to limit the turnover of a position, or portfolio, in fewer than three- to five-year increments.

Portfolio turnover is the measure of the frequency of the buying and selling of assets by the investment manager, whether an individual or professional. Also, gauge institutional portfolio turnover to actively managed ETFs and mutual funds. Low-cost active fund managers keep fees in check by limiting position churns or portfolio turnover. I manage our family's portfolio turnover to between 10 years and eternity. On the contrary, active trading produces excess fees and commissions as well as tax liabilities on short-term capital gains, sabotaging any actual profits from the speculative activity.

Productive investment research involves a simple, straightforward, and consistent, if unexciting, approach to analyzing a targeted business and the underlying stock. The goal of the retail investor on Main Street is to keep portfolio costs super-efficient as if running a small, home-based business.

The Promises and Perils of Common Stock Investing

Long-view investing is the pursuit of the opportunity of total return from compounding capital and dividends—market gyrations notwithstanding—against the perils of the inherent risks and costs of the exercise.

Whether an active or passive investor, it is imperative to keep portfolio costs as economical as possible to amplify returns. And, whether investing in individual stocks, bonds, mutual funds, or exchange-traded funds, cost management is as crucial as the compounding of capital gains and collecting dividend payments.

Unlike the fluctuating capital gains and dividend payouts from company and market gyrations, portfolio expenses are controllable. Opportunities are ever present to keep portfolio costs as low as possible.

* * *

CHAPTER EIGHTEEN SUMMARY

On Controlling Portfolio Costs

- A primary responsibility of the retail-level investor is to run their portfolio as a small, home-based business, keeping investment costs as low as possible.

- Use an online discount broker with a zero-commission structure when buying or selling common stocks or hedging with index ETFs.

■ Beyond the ubiquitous trading commissions and advisory fees, there are other often-overlooked costs to self-directed portfolios, including employer-sponsored retirement plan advisory fees, inflation, income taxes on dividends and capital gains, and subscription fees.

■ Limiting position turnover in a portfolio will decrease costs as well, amplifying an increase in opportunities for the compounding of capital gains and dividend payouts.

■ Despite any underlying genius, professionals charging high fees often parallels underwhelming investment performance. In contrast, self-managing a low-cost portfolio that is outperforming the market over a long-term holding period brings out the investing virtuoso in each of us.

* * *

PART III: PRACTICES

○ What other principles and strategies do you deploy to build and manage a cost-efficient common stock portfolio?

Thank you for joining me in finding value with a margin of safety and building wealth from compounding total return through each market cycle toward financing significant milestones in life.

Buying and holding the dividend-paying common stocks of quality companies at sensible prices remains the most straightforward path to success as an individual retail investor. Construct and maintain an ETF-hedged, concentrated portfolio of common stocks in an attempt to beat the market over time. Accomplish alpha by investing in wonderful companies over enduring periods as opposed to the shortsightedness of trading in and out of faceless stocks.

I dedicate this book to the thoughtful investor committed to continuous portfolio performance improvement and disciplined to conduct the necessary due diligence to discover companies with sound fundamentals whose common shares are trading at attractive valuations, thus demonstrating the propensity for downside protection of capital invested. Patience becomes paramount to portfolio success in waiting through market and company gyrations for the investment theses to play out over a long-term holding period.

A Common Sense Approach

My mission in writing *Build Wealth with Common Stocks* was to educate the everyday retail investor who is passionate about learning, practicing, and sharing in the art and science of profitable self-directed investing. The motivated individual who is willing to overcome the significant challenges of the investment paradigm by keeping investing super simple and allowing common sense to prevail.

Never practice FOMO (the fear of missing out); instead, exercise the more practical FOLM or the fear of losing money because protecting the initial capital invested in your portfolio is priority number one. In the extended post-Great Recession bull market—teetering from the COVID-19 coronavirus pandemic—and occurring during the research and writing of this book, these exceptional value investor attributes were an antithesis to the exuberant Wall Street way and the crowd it influences on Main Street.

During the epic bull market, buy-and-hold value investing appeared out of favor on Wall Street as well as on Main Street. Yet, this time-tested investment practice gives the retail investor an excellent opportunity to fund life's more ambitious goals, such as buying a home, paying for a college education, pursuing a passion, starting a business, or enjoying a comfortable retirement.

While on the journey, relish the experience of owning slices of excellent companies that contribute to socio-economic opportunities for your family, country, and the world. Borrowing from the medieval French poem about the patience required to develop the ancient city of Rome, no one builds a life-changing portfolio in a day.

In the 2020s decade, I will practice what I have learned through trial and error for the past ten plus years in outperforming the market: screen for and research superior, dividend-paying companies trading at value prices, and hold a fractional slice of the business for as long as it remains a quality operator. By equating stock ownership to partnering with the board and employees of the company in providing customers with in-demand products or services from a premise of fundamentals and valuation remains an enduring, profitable, and satisfying way to invest.

The alternatives involve trading in and out of stocks based on technical charts, market sentiment, trend following, momentum growth, high-yield dividends, precision price targets, growth projections, quarterly performance, or any of the noise preached daily on Wall Street, often with dubious outcomes.

Value Prevails Across Market Cycles

My portfolio was outperforming its benchmark, including on the downside by maintaining a wide margin of safety, a critical element of successful value investing. Protect your principal up front against the unpredictable yet unavoidable downturns, and the upside often takes care of itself. Stop making bets on *stocks* and start investing in *companies*.

Once again, mitigate any underlying risks by employing a value-based, long-view portfolio strategy. Hold your shares for as long as the company remains terrific, as demonstrated by growing revenues and earnings, and, more important, by generating free cash flow and capital allocations that produce compounding annual returns for you and your fellow shareholders.

By investing using common sense, you increase your likelihood of getting rich slow, and getting rich slowly is better than not at all.

On Quality vs. Quantity

The challenge of quality over quantity espouses excellence, in theory, often eclipsed by volume in practice. Consider the top TV series, video games, YouTube channels, and movie franchises. What style of content becomes the ratings king more often, quality art or quantitative drivel?

I hope eternal that quality prevails, although, in the end, art gets the awards as drivel pays the bills.

In 20 years of equities investing, I have found that volume drives Wall Street. As a published writer, I have experienced that page views, new followers, comments, and subscriptions increase in tandem with the number of releases. It is the same for investment advisors: volume drives clients and, in turn, drives assets under management. Activity breeds activity.

Perhaps it is similar to viewing a movie or TV show. We dread the content because of questionable quality; however, other viewers are captivated by it because the material makes them feel good. Quality lies in the eye of the beholder, whether viewer, listener or reader. If challenging the producers of a popular television reality series about the show's quality, the response perhaps defends the excellence of the camera work, audio, editing, makeup, and set design. How about the show itself?

The reaction from the showrunner is similar to, "Well, it makes viewers happy, and we have successful ratings as a result."

Investment forums often broach the subject of confirmation bias. How many readers are satisfied, or worse, feel good because a book, article, or podcast confirms a thesis on a stock, industry, or market, regardless of the quality of the content?

The bias occurs more often than we want to believe or admit. For better or worse, we now live in a quantity-driven, confirmation-biased society fed by political ideology, news commentary, entertainment, career success, and personal finance. The demand is for content that confirms our beliefs and values, or we turn our attention elsewhere. In today's media universe, whether video, audio, or written, it is the targeted eyes and ears dictating the quality, perhaps having more of an influence than the producers of the content.

As an example of this paradigm, close to 33 percent of my 70 published articles on the investment site *Seeking Alpha*, posted as Editors' Picks, an esteemed positive confirmation for a contributor. Perhaps you think that I was an oft-read author or top 10 contributor?

I was neither, by a longshot. A terrific and supportive *Seeking Alpha* editorial team encouraged me to write and submit more content more often. The answer to that challenge is this book.

In the global, internet-driven, confirmation-biased culture, the quantity was driving the quality, as opposed to the other way around. On the contrary, a hybrid of qualitative and quantitative investment analysis of a company's present value is more profitable than trading the stock on charts, news, and predictive analysis.

On Growth vs. Value

As in politics, religion, and competitive sports, the paradigm of investing based on the enduring argument of growth versus value divides us. As discussed in Part I: Chapter Nine, dividend-paying value stocks are the polar opposite of non-dividend growth stocks. If an investor is buying high-flying growth stocks for the earnings or dividends, if any, disappointment ensues because the opportunity lies in the top-line growth and free cash flow.

On the other hand, if buying value stocks for hyper-revenue growth, disappointment prevails following each quarterly report. By contrast, the compounding returns from capital gains and dividends continue to reward the patient, value-based investor for years to come.

The recent popularity of non-dividend-paying, ultra-growth stocks was redefining how shares were valued. Perhaps the trend was stuck on the illusion of ever-rising stock prices without regard to valuation multiples and underlying fundamentals. The widespread presumption of the death of value investing as we knew it was a trend in itself. Such a vogue paradigm fades, as trends do, and the argument reverts to the mean of everything is bought and sold based on the correlation between quality and price.

This fundamental economic reality presents in ways both rational and irrational. Still, it never ceases because, in theory, valuation cannot deviate from independent perceptions of the actual price relative to the perceived worth from the buyer and seller.

As an example, imagine you are a partner in a privately held business shedding products that were underselling, therefore yielding slow, no, or negative top-line growth. Instead, the focus shifts to growing newer products with better prospects, still beating the earnings estimates and paying dividends to you and your partners. Are you dumping your share of the partnership as growth and momentum investors often do as a matter of practice?

The answer is no if you were confident in the opportunities that lie ahead. Nevertheless, as noninstitutional investors, we lack the activist clout to influence change in the boardroom. The quest for total return lies in the fundamentals of a company and the valuation of the underlying stock. We want to own quality, customer-focused, shareholder-friendly companies that are efficient capital allocators and whose stock is available at a reasonable price at the time of purchase.

On Wall Street vs. Main Street

To risk sounding like a broken record with good intentions, I enjoy teaching or reminding fellow retail-level investors the surest way to sustain investment success is to keep it super simple with a pinch of common sense.

For better or worse, our common sense and instinct become the leading indicators for predicting the general direction of future company performance and stock prices. The Wall Street way tells us it is hogwash as it cannot monetize common sense and instinct into a deep-dive sell-side research report or buy-side quarterly note to clients. In contrast, by reading 10-Ks and listening to live earnings calls and annual shareholder meetings, the individual investor on Main Street gauges the worthiness of being a part owner of the business, assuming the fundamentals and valuations are favorable.

The modern trend on Wall Street is seeking information unbaked into the price of the security. Find something no one else knows—albeit nonmaterial, public information yet to reach the market en masse—and manipulate the data to a legal advantage. Walking the line runs counter to the wisdom of the value investor on Main Street who enjoys the thrill of victory or accepts the agony of defeat after consummation of the investment, albeit never before or during the trade.

Look for companies you have confidence in by investing your hard-earned dollars as a partial owner of the enterprise. Wall Street seems to make its money on the fees, commissions, and assets under management float generated from the so-called "can't miss" ideas. Moreover, the club keeps this knowledge privy for insiders with genetically induced high IQs and college fraternity-driven connections.

On the other side of the abyss, the value-based investor on Main Street practices intelligent, patient, long-term, and low-cost investing. Plenty of reliable public information is available to generate potential returns from the common stock itself as opposed to the fees and bonuses generated from self-aggrandizing hypotheses.

From diligent research, although a stock appears undervalued, the informed investor on Main Street never becomes swayed by the illusion of the ability to predict exact percentages of pricing discrepancies. Remember, if the procrastinators were more often right—wrong, being the typical outcome—the so-called 1 percent of wealth becomes more like the top 50 percent.

A Passion for Building Wealth with Common Stocks

Do-it-yourself, retail-level investing must be a passion or serious hobby for any chance of success over the long term. On the other side, passive investing is ideal for individual investors uncomfortable or uninterested in actively investing or paying high fees to money managers.

Part I: Chapter Eight showed that a passive, diversified, low-fee portfolio of indexed mutual or exchange-traded funds, by design, averages to the market. The passive investor must resolve to average results on both the upside and the downside.

And that is the premise of how *Build Wealth with Common Stocks* and The Model Portfolio operate. Have respect for the low-cost, less-risk foundation of index investing that John Bogle advocated for decades, and aspire to the gratification and potential rewards of Warren Buffett-style active investing, albeit with limited capital. Although some of the risk aversion is compromised, the self-directed investor who enjoys researching and owning publicly traded common shares of businesses still enjoys low-cost active investing.

Self-Driving Cars and Portfolios

As far as the ever-present machine-driven investment paradigms, including quantitative algorithms and high-frequency trading, those are built for speculators interested in casino high-roller kinds of returns from the stock market. Just as at the casino, the house wins more often on Wall Street. Nonetheless, these algorithmic technologies may one day reach universal availability beyond the burgeoning, automated, inhuman robo-advisors now in play, thus allowing the do-it-yourself investor to download cost-efficient cloud-based software to screen, research, trade, and monitor value-based, buy-and-hold portfolios of quality, publicly traded companies and ETF index hedges.

Envision a future of self-driving cars and self-driving individual portfolios, with online platforms as an integral part of the essential portfolio toolbox available in the cloud for the retail-level investor.

Make the Tough Choices — Then Proceed with Care

The thoughtful investor owns risk-averse slices of wonderful companies, thereby leaving the trading of stocks to risk-defying speculators. Practice quantitative investment research within a model driving to a qualitative outcome of a bullish, neutral, or bearish call on the targeted company and the stock representing public ownership. Bring forth the benefit of an individual investor approach focused on buying slices of companies rather than having an index or active fund manager pick and choose the holdings. Make the tough choices and take personal responsibility when clicking the buy or sell trade button at your online discount broker.

CEOs and societal woes come and go. Although the mispriced stocks of magnificent capital-deploying companies present rare opportunities in every market, each is never devoid of risk. Investing in common shares is the proverbial double-edged sword of participating in socioeconomic empowerment by owning slices of companies perpetuating greed from the trading of stocks. Increase your chances of being right more often than wrong by staying thoughtful, disciplined, and patient. Plus, equal-weighting your portfolio increases the likelihood of outperformance by limiting conscious and subconscious bias.

Proceed with care, remembering the benefits of physical and emotional health far outweigh any advantages of financial wealth. Life on Earth is indeed fleeting, and none of us are getting out of here alive. In that kindred spirit, I close the book with words of infinite wisdom from the narrator in the movie *Fight Club*, adapted from Chuck Palahniuk's best-selling satirical novel of the same title. It is indeed a sobering reminder to never delay pursuing what is important.

> " *On a long enough timeline, the survival rate for everyone* "
> *drops to zero.*[1]

Hence, we won't be trading shares as an anointed member of the departed. Nevertheless, the thoughtful, disciplined, and patient common stock investor looks forward and beyond knowing that a legacy portfolio comprising the slices of quality, enduring enterprises continues to compound in the appreciative hands of loved ones.

* * *

EPILOGUE SUMMARY
On Becoming a Thoughtful, Disciplined, and Patient Investor

- Find value with a margin of safety and build wealth from compounding total return on capital gains and dividends across each market cycle.

- Outperform Wall Street from your perch on Main Street with a common stock portfolio built and maintained on simple principles and strategies with a pinch of common sense.

- Remember, price and value prevail in every area of our economic lives, including the stock market.

- Prevent confirmation bias—the debilitating heart and soul of the contemporary media paradigm—from clouding your investing judgment. Stay true to you by investing with wisdom and integrity in a world discounting honesty to its peril.

- Invest with thought, discipline, and patience, remembering the benefits of physical and emotional health outweigh any advantages of financial wealth.

RESURCES ▌

The following resources for individual investors were curated from the author's personal experiences and are suggestions for further research and education.

Books

Browne, Christopher H. *The Little Book of Value Investing*. Hoboken, NJ: John Wiley & Sons 2006.

Collins, Jim. *Good to Great*. New York: Harper Business, 2001.

Graham, Benjamin. *The Intelligent Investor*. New York: HarperCollins, 1949.

Graham, Benjamin, Dodd, David L. *Security Analysis*. New York: McGraw-Hill, 1934.

Greenblatt, Joel. *You Can Be a Stock Market Genius*. New York: Simon & Schuster, 1997.

Hagstrom, Robert G. *The Warren Buffett Way*. Hoboken, NJ: John Wiley & Sons, 2013.

Lewis, Michael. *Liar's Poker*. New York: W.W. Norton & Company, 1989.

Lynch, Peter, Rothchild, John. *Beating the Street*. New York: Simon & Schuster, 1994.

Lynch, Peter, Rothchild, John. *One Up On Wall Street*. New York: Simon & Schuster, 1989.

Marks, Howard. *The Most Important Thing*. New York: Columbia University Press, 2011.

Smith, Adam. *The Wealth of Nations*. London: Strahan and Cadell, 1776.

Tian, Charlie. *Invest Like a Guru*. Hoboken, NJ: John Wiley & Sons, 2017.

Film

Becoming Warren Buffett. Director: Peter Kunhardt. HBO Documentary Films, 2017.

Letters

Buffett, Warren E. "Letters to Shareholders, Berkshire Hathaway, Inc." berkshirehathaway.com/letters/letters.html (1977-2019).

Marks, Howard. "Memos from Howard Marks." Oaktree Capital Management, LP. oaktreecapital.com/insights/howard-marks-memos (1990-2020).

Websites

Brokers

Charles Schwab & Co.: https://www.schwab.com

E*Trade Financial: https://us.etrade.com

Fidelity Investments: https://www.fidelity.com

Robinhood Markets: https://robinhood.com/us/en

The Vanguard Group: https://investor.vanguard.com

Calculators

Income Tax: http://www.tax-rates.org

Inflation: https://www.usinflationcalculator.com

Financial: https://www.timevalue.com/tcalc-financial-calculators

Content

Seeking Alpha: https://seekingalpha.com

TalkMarkets: https://talkmarkets.com

Tools

Google Finance: https://www.google.com/finance

GuruFocus: https://www.gurufocus.com

Mint: https://www.mint.com

Morningstar: https://www.morningstar.com

The Model Portfolio: https://davidjwaldron.com/index.html

Yahoo Finance: https://finance.yahoo.com

NOTES

Chapter One

1. Merriam-Webster, s.v. "value," accessed July 1, 2020, https://www.merriam-webster.com/dictionary/value.

Chapter Two

1. Tom Herman, "Weekend Report—'How to Profit from Economists' Forecasts,'" *The Wall Street Journal*, January 22, 1993, C1.
2. Warren E. Buffett, Berkshire Hathaway, Inc., *2013 Letter to Shareholders*, February 28, 2014, 20.*
3. *Wall Street*, directed by Oliver Stone (Century City, CA: 20th Century Studios, 1987).

Chapter Three

1. Yahoo Finance, "AAPL, Historical Data, Prices, Stock Splits, Dividends" accessed September 8, 2020, https://finance.yahoo.com/quote/AAPL.
2. The Coca-Cola Company, "Historical Data," accessed July 2, 2020, https://investors.coca-colacompany.com/stock-information/historical-data.
3. Warren E. Buffett, 2003 Berkshire Hathaway, Inc. annual shareholder meeting (answer to audience question #41), https://buffett.cnbc.com/video/2003/05/03/businesses-with-ideal-financial-traits-are-hard-to-come-by.html.*
4. Benjamin Graham, *The Intelligent Investor* (New York: Harper-Collins, 1949).

5. *Becoming Warren Buffett*, directed by Peter Kunhardt (New York: Kunhardt Films, HBO Documentary Films, 2017).

Chapter Five

1. Warren E. Buffett, Berkshire Hathaway, Inc., *1987 Letter to Shareholders*, February 29, 1988.*
2. Evelyn Cheng, "The Stock Market is Officially in a Correction...Here's What Usually Happens Next," CNBC, February 8, 2018, https://www.cnbc.com/2018/02/08/the-stock-market-is-officially-in-a-correction-heres-what-usually-happens-next.html.

Chapter Six

1. Peter Lynch and John Rothchild, *Beating the Street* (New York: Simon & Schuster, 1993, 1994), 305.
2. Howard Marks, *The Most Important Thing* (New York: Columbia University Press, 2011), 19–20, original quote published in Marks's memo to clients of Oaktree Capital Management, L.P.: "The Happy Medium," July 21, 2004.

Chapter Eight

1. Warren E. Buffett, Berkshire Hathaway, Inc., *2002 Letter to Shareholders*, February 21, 2003, 15.*
2. Howard Marks, *The Most Important Thing* (New York: Columbia University Press, 2011), 97, original quote published in Marks's memo to clients of Oaktree Capital Management, L.P.: "The Limits to Negativism," October 15, 2008.

Chapter Ten

1. Benjamin Graham and David L. Dodd, *Security Analysis*, Sixth Edition (New York: McGraw-Hill, 2009, 1934).

2. Warren E. Buffett, Berkshire Hathaway, Inc., *2008 Letter to Shareholders*, February 27, 2009, 5.*

3. Seeking Alpha, "SA Interview: Investing for the Long-Term with Belgian and Bullish," February 10, 2018, https://seekingalpha.com/article/4144881-sa-interview-investing-for-long-term-belgian-and-bullish.

Chapter Eleven

1. Peter Lynch and John Rothchild, *Beating the Street* (New York: Simon & Schuster, 1993, 1994), 27.

2. Drake Baer, "How Nike Got An Insane Deal on The 'Swoosh' Logo," Business Insider, July 25, 2014, https://www.businessinsider.com/nike-bought-swoosh-logo-for-35-2014-7.

Chapter Thirteen

1. Jim Collins, *Good to Great* (New York: Harper Business, 2001), 20.

Chapter Fourteen

1. Howard Marks, *The Most Important Thing* (New York: Columbia University Press, 2011), 27, original quote published in Marks's memo to clients of Trust Company of the West: "Random Thoughts on the Identification of Investment Opportunities," January 24, 1994.

Chapter Fifteen

1. Howard Marks, *The Most Important Thing* (New York: Columbia University Press, 2011), x.

Chapter Sixteen

1. Peter Lynch and John Rothchild, *One Up On Wall Street* (New York: Simon & Schuster, 1989).

Chapter Eighteen

1. InflationData.com, "Average Annual Inflation Rates by Decade," accessed September 1, 2020, https://inflationdata.com/inflation/inflation/decadeinflation.asp.
2. Tax Policy Center, "Statistics," accessed September 1, 2020, https://www.taxpolicycenter.org/statistics/individual.
3. Warren E. Buffett, Berkshire Hathaway, Inc., *1996 Letter to Shareholders*, February 28, 1997.*

Epilogue

1. *Fight Club*, directed by David Fincher (Century City, CA: 20th Century Studios, 1999). Based on the novel by Chuck Palahniuk, *Fight Club* (New York: W.W. Norton & Company, 1996).

* * *

*Material is copyrighted and used with the permission of the author.

ABOUT THE AUTHOR

David J. Waldron is an individual investor and the author of self-improvement books for those seeking to achieve the personal and professional goals that matter most in their life.

In addition to *Build Wealth with Common Stocks*, David has written three other nonfiction books. *Hire Train Monitor Motivate* offers practical career-building strategies toward improving organization, team, or individual career achievements in the hyper-competitive local and global marketplaces. *The Ten Domains of Effective Goal Setting* provides a workable template with a simple, holistic, and attainable objective toward a happier and more rewarding life, whether at home, school, play, or the workplace. *A Great Place to Learn & Earn* is David's professional memoir as a former 25-year veteran of postsecondary career education.

He is working with his wife, Suzan, on her memoir, *One of a Million Faces*, about living and coping with Type 1 diabetes and its complications.

David earned a Bachelor of Science in business studies as a Garden State Scholar at Stockton University and completed The Practice of Management Program at Brown University. He and Suzan reside in historic South Central Pennsylvania, USA.

Take control and achieve your dreams at davidjwaldron.com.

Made in the USA
Columbia, SC
12 April 2022

58874339R10124